STITCHED GIFTS

STITCHED GIFTS

25 SWEET AND SIMPLE EMBROIDERY PROJECTS FOR EVERY OCCASION

By Jessica Marquez

CHRONICLE BOOKS

SAN FRANCISCO

Library of Congress Cataloging-in-Publication Data:
Marquez, Jessica.
Stitched gifts : 25 sweet and simple embroidery projects
for every occasion / by Jessica Marquez.
pages cm
Includes index.
ISBN 978-1-4521-0726-4
1. Embroidery – Patterns. I. Title.
TT771.M34 2012
746.44 – dc23
2011053144

Manufactured in China
Designed by Vivien Sung
Typeset by Graeme Jones
Photographs by Jessica Marquez
Additional Retouching by Jeremy Dyer

Bohin is a registered trademark of Bohin France Société Anonyme.
Clover is a registered trademark of Clover Mfg. Co., Ltd. Delta Creative
and Sobo are registered trademarks of Delta Technical Coatings, Inc.
DMC Creative World is a registered trademark of Dollfus Mief & Cie.
Electric Quilt is a registered trademark of Electric Quilt Co. Fray Check
is a registered trademark of General Dispersions Inc. iDye is a registered
trademark of Rupert, Gibbon & Spider, Inc. IKEA is a registered
trademark of Inter IKEA Systems B.V. Besloten Vennootschap. Kobalt
is a registered trademark of LF, LLC. Lineco is a registered tratdemark
of Lineco, Inc. Loew-Cornell is a registered trademark of Loew-
Cornell, Inc. Mod Podge is a registered trademark of Enterprise Paint
Manufacturing Co. Pellon and Stitch-n-Tear are registered trademarks
of Pellon Corp. Sajou is a registered trademark of Frederique Crestin
Billet. Saral is a registered trademark of Saral Paper Co., Inc. Sharpie
is a registered trademark of Sanford. Solvy is a registered trademark
of Gunold USA, Inc. Sobo is a registered trademark of Delta Creative,
Inc. Stiffy is a registered trademark of Plaid Enterprises, Inc. Sulky is a
registered trademark of Gunold + Stickma Materials GMBH Co. Thread
Heaven is a registered trademark of Donna L. Hennen. Wonder-Under
is a registered trademark of Freudenberg Nonwovens Ltd. X-ACTO is a
registered trademark of Elmer's Products, Inc.

10 9 8 7 6 5 4 3 2 1

Chronicle Books LLC
680 Second Street
San Francisco, California 94107
www.chroniclebooks.com

To my parents, Rod and Cici, who have always supported me and encouraged me to pursue a creative path

Acknowledgments

Thom O'Hearn got this whole ball rolling; a big thank you to him for seeing the potential in my work. Much appreciation and thanks to Lindsay Edgecombe, whose constant support throughout this process has been invaluable. Thank you to all at Chronicle, especially Laura Lee Mattingly, who thoughtfully guided this book into being, and Allison Weiner for photography guidance and design.

To Jeremy Dyer, who helped me at every step with kindness, patience, and endless cups of tea, thank you.

Big hugs and big thanks to some of the craftiest ladies around: Michelle Cavigliano, Julie Schneider, and Virginia Kraljevic. Michelle and Julie, thank you for your helpful read through and edits. Virginia's home is filled with amazing vintage finds (see Home & Hearth image, pages 34–35), and I was lucky enough to shoot some pictures in her home. Thanks so much for your styling and photo help.

Some of the pictures in this book were taken in the lovely Brooklyn apartment of my friends Becky Hurwitz and Adam Ryder; thanks so much guys!

Thank you so much to Erin Hunt and Kingsman Brewster for letting me photograph your beautiful daughter, Ingrid.

To all the people who have supported my work, at Miniature Rhino and otherwise, you make me happy and I am thankful.

To you! Thank you for reading this book.

CONTENTS

INTRODUCTION

In college I spent most of my time holed up in a tiny darkroom developing film, printing black-and-white negatives, and processing color prints. I liked the smell of fixative on my hands, flipping on the light of the enlarger revealing a ghostly projected image in the dark, and the formulaic steps of it all. But the thing I liked most was watching an image appear on photographic paper after being exposed to light. I'd gently rock the paper back and forth in the tray of developer and, like magic, the image would come forth. I come back to that moment of an image slowly developing, appearing from nothing, when I think of embroidery. It's a process that unfolds with time, stitch by stitch making magic.

Unexpectedly, it was photography that brought me to embroidery. While working on a master's in imaging arts at Rochester Institute of Technology, I stumbled into working with needle and thread. I was creating a miniature museum of my family and had worked with a geneticist to code my family's DNA. I decided to portray the scrolling code of DNA by embroidering it, and began teaching myself embroidery with old library books. I did everything wrong in the beginning—I didn't wash my fabrics first and ended up shrinking my fabric and my stitches into a blob of thread; I used pencil to make patterns, which never washes out (but I kind of like that!); and I made lots of mistakes (I still do, and you will too).

One of the reasons I love embroidery so much is because it is so forgiving. You can learn the "right" way to make a stitch, but every one of us will make it a little bit different. The length of the stitch, just where your needle enters the fabric, how tight you pull your thread, even the colors you choose and the style of your work—it all differs from person to person. I liken embroidery to drawing or painting. It can be loose and expressive, built up in layers, or just a mark here and there. Even when a pattern or a particularly precise stitch is involved, there are so many ways to make it your own. Forgive me here, cross-stitch, but you are just not as satisfying—so rigid, so mathematical, so few options. My heart belongs to embroidery.

Believe it or not, I've never used a commercial embroidery pattern. I've always made my own, simply because I enjoy creating personalized pieces. Almost all of the embroideries I've made for my online shop, Miniature Rhino, are custom, given as gifts for weddings, birthdays, new babies, and the like. I saw that people wanted unique, handmade gifts that were personal and made with love, but not cheesy. The twenty-five patterns in this book are made with this—and you—in mind. Here is a collection of gift-worthy projects with a twist of nostalgia and Victorian romanticism that will whet your appetite for embroidery, and give you lots of wiggle room to customize. Whatever the occasion, there is a project in here for you, even if it's something to make "just because"!

But, before you jump into the projects, I want to get a little personal—this book is all about it! Many of the projects are customizable: you can add your own text, names, a quote, or a date. The idea is to use the perforated printed pattern templates and alphabet templates found at the back of the book to create your own custom patterns. These templates are ready to use, but they can also be scanned, enlarged, reduced, saved, and printed as many times as you like. I also explain how to create your own custom patterns.

The first step in embroidery is transferring patterns onto fabric. You are probably familiar with iron-on transfers, but these leave you with little wiggle room to modify the pattern. With the projects in this book, I want you to have as much flexibility as possible, so that you can change the size, even change the lines of the template if you like, and add your own details. So first, I show you different transfer techniques that I use, and then you can figure out what works best for you. Then I take you through the steps of each individual project with detailed instructions. For many of the projects, I offer options for simplifying steps. And you can also always forgo the alphabet templates by adding your own freehand text. For each project, I've provided the approximate length of time that it takes to make it. The times will vary depending on your choices, but all of the projects can be made in a weekend.

Every project in this book was cooked up in my Brooklyn studio (a.k.a. the spare bedroom) during an intensely hot summer. I felt like a mad scientist, working away in my craft lab at all hours of the night and day, getting the details just right. All of these embroidery projects were created so that you can

make memorable gifts for someone special, or for yourself. My hope is that these projects excite your imagination, challenge and develop your skills, give you lots of creative inspiration, and provide many days of enjoyable making.

– Jessica Marquez

TOOLS & MATERIALS

One thing I love about embroidery is that you don't need much to start. With just an embroidery hoop, fabric, scissors, and needle and thread, you're ready to stitch. These tools and materials are pretty inexpensive too. If you're going to splurge on something, though, I'd suggest good-quality fabric scissors, small sharp snips, and linen fabric. I've suggested here my favorite supplies and materials to work with, all of which can easily be found in any craft store (see Resources, page 134). Some of these projects do push the boundaries of the usual embroidery toolbox though: for example, you'll have some fun with craft wire, Wonder Under, and fabric stiffener.

Embroidery Thread

There are many types of embroidery thread, including pearl cotton, stranded and nondivisible thread, embroidery yarn, and tapestry wool. Thread can be made from satin, silk, linen, wool, and even soy. Each has a unique appearance and texture, and provides different embroidered effects.

My favorite thread, and what I use throughout this book, is DMC stranded cotton embroidery floss. It is widely available, comes in every imaginable color, and is versatile to work with. This thread has six strands, or plies (rather than one strand, or ply), which can be easily separated to create stitches of varying thicknesses. (Nondivisible thread has a single ply.) DMC thread is available in many different styles, even satin, metallic, and glow-in-the-dark.

Let's just get an issue out there: Embroidery thread will be your best friend and can be your worst enemy at times. Threads that knot, tangle, and fray can drive you crazy. The best way to tame them is to cut shorter lengths of thread to work with (about 14 to 24 in/ 35.5 to 61 cm), snip away any fraying thread ends right away, and let your thread "unwind" periodically while you are working. To unwind your thread, let your working thread and needle dangle from the fabric. Once it has uncoiled itself, then you're ready to stitch again. If you find your threads just don't want to cooperate, save yourself the headache and just put on a new length of thread. You can also try using a thread conditioner like Thread Heaven, to smooth out threads.

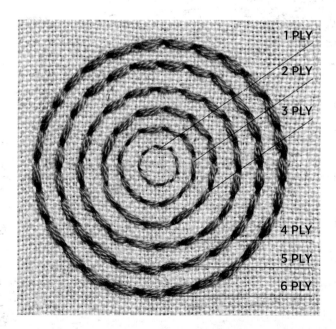

1 PLY
2 PLY
3 PLY
4 PLY
5 PLY
6 PLY

To easily separate stranded thread into sections, pinch one end of thread about ½ in/12 mm from the end. Tap the thread and watch the plies separate. Separate the strands into the desired plies and slowly pull one finger through the two sections. The strands will want to rewind, so make sure to keep the sections of thread separate.

TIP: To thread a needle: I think most of us are familiar with the lick method for threading a needle, which works well, but do you want to be licking your thread all the time? Here is another great, easy method I use: I make a small loop with the thread around the needle. Pinch the loop around the needle between your thumb and pointer finger, and pull the loop tight to form a point in the thread. Slide the needle out, then push that little looped point through the eye of the needle. Your thread can't be thicker than the needle eye, and should be nice and smooth.

Fabric

I prefer natural fabrics for embroidering—cotton and linen are my favorites. Linen is my go-to fabric of choice. Muslin is a loosely woven inexpensive cotton fabric that is nice to work with, especially for practicing your stitches. Synthetic fabrics or fabrics with lots of stretch are more difficult to work with, but not impossible. With the help of some stabilizer, stretchy fabrics are much easier to work with. You can stitch on practically anything.

When choosing a fabric, consider the weave. The weave of a fabric describes the vertical (warp) and horizontal (weft) threads of the fabric. The tighter the weave of the fabric, the more difficult it will be to work with, because it's more difficult to pull a needle and thread through a tight fabric. A more open weave, like linen, is easy and smooth to work with.

Before you begin embroidering, prepare your fabric. Wash and preshrink your fabric, especially if you will be washing the finished embroidery. I was so disappointed after I washed a pillowcase that I had spent hours embroidering without washing first. It shrank and distorted my stitches into a mess. If you are pressed for time and the fabric is not going to be washed, you can saturate the fabric with water from a spray bottle and iron it dry.

TIP: Fabric care: For finished pieces that will be displayed in hoops, you really don't need to do much to clean them. Spot clean or use a lint roller, if needed. For other types of finished work, you should probably hand-wash them. Never wring an embroidered piece, instead hang it or lay it flat to dry. Iron the piece from the back side of the fabric or under a damp cloth.

Needles

To keep it simple, I use two needle sizes throughout this book, sizes 5 and 7 embroidery needles. In general, the larger the number, the smaller the needle. So the size 5 needle is better suited for thicker, 6-ply thread while the smaller, size 7 needle is better for thinner threads with fewer plies. There are many different types of needles—chenille, crewel, embroidery, tapestry, sharps, quilting—all for different uses. The lengths of the needles, sharpness of the points, and size of the needle eyes vary depending on the use. I find that chenille, crewel, and embroidery needles are the best for embroidery work. They all have sharp points, roomy needle eyes, and convenient needle lengths that aren't too short. If you're having trouble threading a standard embroidery needle, try a chenille or crewel needle. The chenille needle has a long, oval eye and the crewel needle has a wide eye made for thick wool thread.

Scissors

I use different scissors for paper, fabric, and thread. General craft scissors are used for cutting paper and stabilizer. Fabric scissors are sharp, and cut fabric like butter. They can be expensive, so to keep them in good condition I only use them on fabric. My thread scissors, or snips, have a fine, precise point so that I can cut threads close to the fabric.

Hoops

Throughout the book, I use wooden embroidery hoops to frame finished projects. These hoops, both circular and oval, range from 3 to 10 in/7.5 to 25 cm in diameter. I've found most of these hoops in thrift stores and antique shops. I usually use plastic hoops when I stitch, which feel sturdier and hold the fabric

taut longer than wooden hoops. It's really a personal preference, as both plastic and wood hoops do the job. Remove the hoop from your embroidery piece when you're not working on it to prevent hoop marks.

> TIP: A general rule of the thumb for sizing your fabric to match your hoop size, add 2 in/5 cm to the diameter. So, if you have a 3-in/7.5-cm hoop, you'll need a piece of fabric that is 5 in/12.5 cm square.

To mount fabric into an embroidery hoop, it helps to have a clean, flat, sturdy work surface. Place your fabric over the inner ring of the embroidery hoop, which should be lying flat on your work surface. The fabric's weave should be lined up horizontally and vertically in front of you. On the outer hoop ring, tighten the hardware so that the hoop just fits around the fabric and the inner hoop. Apply even pressure over the outer hoop ring and press down, so that it slides over the fabric and inner ring. Smooth any bumps or wrinkles by pulling gently on the fabric edges. The fabric surface in the hoop should be flat, smooth, and taut. The trick is to get the tension just right without distorting the fabric weave or the transferred pattern.

Stabilizers

Stabilizer is interfacing used on the reverse side of the embroidered fabric. It helps prevent fabric, especially thin or stretchy fabric, from distorting when you hoop it, and it provides a sturdier work surface. There are many kinds of stabilizers: water-soluble, ink-jet printable, sticky backed, heat-soluble, tear-away, and permanent. My preferred brand is Sulky—it works great and they have a dizzying selection of stabilizers to choose from. I mainly use two types: a permanent, heavy stabilizer as a backing to strengthen the fabric I'm embroidering (Sulky Stiffy—no joke, that's the name, or Pellon Stitch-N-Tear); and a thin, semitransparent, temporary stabilizer (Sulky Tear-Easy), which I use as a transfer medium. Experiment with different stabilizers to find out what works best for you.

I often use the permanent stabilizer as a backing for my fabric when embroidering. It is not necessary to use it, but I find it extremely helpful because it provides a firm surface to stitch on and it can be left on the back of the piece. This option is best for work that will be mounted in a hoop or frame, or for clothing embellishments like on T-shirts. (If you use stabilizer as a backing for clothing, tear away the edges after completing the embroidery so it doesn't rub against the skin.) I do not suggest this option for items that you'll see the back of, like tea towels or pillowcases. In these cases, a water-soluble stabilizer or none at all is best. An alternative to stabilizer is another layer of fabric for the back of a stitched area, and thin cotton works well.

To mount the stabilizer and the fabric in the embroidery hoop, cut a piece of stabilizer to match the size of your fabric piece. Layer the stabilizer under the fabric and over the inner embroidery ring. Place the outer embroidery hoop over the fabric and push down. Gently pull the edges of the fabric and stabilizer smooth, but be careful not to pop off the embroidery hoop. If your stabilizer is thick, it may resist the embroidery hoop a bit. Once the hoop is on, both the fabric and stabilizer should be smooth and taut.

Marking Tools

Water-soluble pens and pencils, dressmaker's chalk, and Sharpies are a must for creating and transferring patterns. General-purpose pencils and erasers and fine-point Sharpies are all you'll need for tracing a template.

Water-soluble pens and pencils are best with light- to medium-colored fabrics. They come in a variety of colors, and disappear when sprayed with water or rubbed gently with a damp cloth. I prefer the pen to the chalky pencil, but the pencils come in light colors that are good for marking dark fabrics. Disappearing ink is air- and water-soluble and will disappear in about two days. My favorite water-soluble pen is Clover Water Soluble Marker (thick).

Dressmaker's chalk or even regular chalk is great for marking dark fabrics, and rubs out easily. For marking long lines on fabric, I often use a chalk wheel, a sewing tool used to make fine, straight lines that can be easily rubbed out.

I'm not a big fan of iron-on transfer pens, but these pens easily transfer patterns traced onto paper and can be ironed onto fabric. You can often use the paper to iron onto fabric multiple times.

A tracing stylus is a useful tool for transferring patterns from printed templates. The stylus has a rounded edge that allows you to apply pressure without ripping the printed template. Use the stylus in combination with transfer paper to easily transfer patterns. You can also use a dried-out pen or a dull pencil.

Thread Conditioner

Thread Heaven is a great conditioner for taming and smoothing thread. It's not necessary to use it all the time, but it is particularly helpful for that one little thread that won't stay in place, for calming strands that you have just separated, or when you are stitching through coarse materials. It's especially useful when stitching paper. Give it a try with the stitched paper projects in this book. Beeswax is another great option.

Sewing Pins

Standard sewing pins are used to pin appliqué pieces and transfer material to your fabric. You can also use extra embroidery needles for pinning.

Glue

I use fabric glue to attach fabric to an embroidery hoop after I've completed a project and am ready to display it. My favorites are Sobo and Lineco Neutral pH Adhesive. The Sobo glue dries clear, won't yellow, and has lots of applications beyond just fabric. It does dry darker, so be careful not to get it on your embroidery. Lineco Neutral pH Adhesive is acid free, archival, and will not yellow or become brittle. Mod Podge is perfect for sealing paper and for collage work. We use it on one project in this book, but you'll be able to find lots of other uses for it.

Rotary Blade

To cut exact edges and precise corners, I suggest using a rotary blade and metal ruler. The rotary blade is crazy sharp, so be careful! When cutting with a rotary blade, use a ruler and always cut the fabric on the side of the ruler that is opposite to any embroidery work, so that if your hand slips it won't cut your stitches.

Tape

Painter's tape is another one of those strange tools that I use nearly every day. I use it to secure my fabric and templates to my work surface so they don't slip while I'm tracing. The tape forms a great hold, but won't rip your paper pattern. And a little strip goes a long way: you can reuse the tape over and over again.

Linen tape is archival, it won't yellow, and is great for mounting finished pieces in mats. Artist's tape can work in a pinch, but I find that it gets brittle over time. Try Lineco Linen Tape.

Stretched Canvas, Canvas Stretcher Bars & Wood Artist Panels

For the projects that I wanted to mount in something other than an embroidery hoop but not in a frame—for example, the Baby Banner Sampler (page 89), and Crossed Arrows & Banner pieces (page 57)—I stretched the embroidered fabric over premade canvas stretcher bars or wood artist panels. These are both painter's materials that you can find at any art supply store. The wood panels, my preferred method, are sturdy, and raise the embroidery from the wall. If you're using canvas stretcher bars, consider using a premade canvas and stretching your embroidery over the canvas. This way the embroidery back is concealed and has a sturdy backing. Use a staple gun to stretch and attach the fabric to the wood.

Staple Gun

A small, general craft staple gun works well for stretching and attaching your finished embroidery pieces over canvas stretcher bars or wood artist panels.

Wonder Under

Wonder Under (or any fusible material) fuses to fabric with an iron and has a peel-away paper backing. (No need for the Heavy-Duty Wonder Under.) Wonder Under is light enough to stitch right through. It is mainly used to create appliqué pieces, but can also be used as a nonremovable stabilizer.

Paper

Tracing paper is very helpful for tracing patterns and adding custom text to your pattern. White printer paper works fine for drawing and sketching patterns. You can use freezer paper as an alternative to Wonder Under and to cover your work surface. Ink-jet Iron-on Transfer Paper and Printable Fabric Paper are used in a few projects in the book.

Fray Check

Fray Check is a clear liquid used to prevent fabric edges from fraying. You can find it in the notions section of sewing and quilting stores. It is used in a few projects in the book as a sealer for raw fabric edges. It's clear, but it can cause some fabrics to dry a bit darker where it is applied. Use it sparingly. In a pinch, you can try clear nail polish, which will stiffen fabric edges but will also darken the fabric.

Iron

A standard iron is needed for ironing fabric and creating appliqué pieces. No need for anything too fancy, just an iron with a few heat settings and a steam option is helpful for smoothing wrinkled fabric.

Bone Folder

A bone folder is a traditional bookbinding tool used to score and smooth papers, and a handy crafting tool too. It has a dull point for marking paper. It can be made of actual bone or synthetic material, which I prefer.

Tweezers

An everyday pair of tweezers will be helpful for removing bits of stabilizer that has been used as a transfer medium.

Ruler

Every craft toolbox needs a metal ruler or two for measuring, marking, and cutting straight lines. I prefer metal rulers, so I can use them with sharp rotary blades without damaging the ruler. Clear plastic rulers are also useful when creating templates, so you can see your previous marks.

TRANSFERRING & PERSONALIZING PATTERNS

The projects in the book are all about adding your own customizations. The basic templates were created so that you can use them as is or modify them to make your own versions. There are many ways to transfer your patterns. Here are several different techniques and the pros and cons of each. These methods will work for creating your very own patterns too.

Many of the projects in the book use two templates—an image template and an alphabet template. Before you can transfer a pattern onto your fabric, you need to create your personalized pattern combining the two templates. If you want to use the printed templates again, I suggest that you photocopy or scan the templates, and print them out so you can draw on the copy to add your custom text and details. You can also use tracing paper to combine the two templates. Once your pattern is complete, you can transfer it to your fabric.

TIP: A general rule of the thumb for sizing your embroidery pattern: Subtract ¾ in/2 cm from the embroidery hoop size for the final pattern size. For example, for a 3-in/7.5-cm hoop, the final pattern size should be 2¼ in/5.5 cm. This decrease in size is an adjustment for the inner hoop ring.

Tear-Away Stabilizer

For this transfer method, use Sulky Tear-Easy, or a light T-shirt stabilizer. You do not need to first create a tracing paper pattern with this method, which can save time. Usually, this material is used under your fabric, but here we use it on top of your fabric as a light, transparent transfer medium. This may seem a bit strange, because you will stitch through the stabilizer over your fabric. But I use this method all the time, because it is fast and easy. Just trace your pattern onto the tear-away material, pin it with sewing pins onto your stretched fabric in the hoop, and stitch just as you normally would.

Some T-shirt stabilizers iron onto the fabric, in which case you first trace the pattern onto the stabilizer, iron the stabilizer onto the fabric, and then hoop the fused stabilizer and fabric.

WHY YOU MIGHT LOVE IT: This method is a great one for transferring images onto dark fabric and stretchy fabric. You can trace your design directly onto the stabilizer, with no need to first make a traced paper pattern. Because the material is transparent, it is easy to trace and combine multiple templates, which is perfect for adding custom text. Also, the method allows your pattern to be transferred without any stretching or distortion.

WHAT YOU MIGHT NOT LIKE ABOUT IT: It might take you a while to get used to stitching through a surface other than your fabric. Once your piece is stitched, removing the material can be a bit tricky, because you need to take your time removing the stabilizer paper. Pulling too hard or fast can lift up your stitches. I cut the stabilizer around the stitches, then I hold the stitches with my fingers and gently pull the stabilizer up. For delicate areas, I cut as close to the stitches as possible and use tweezers to pick away the stabilizer. This method is not the best one for a piece with a lot of satin stitching, because it is difficult to remove stabilizer from underneath satin stitches without disturbing them.

ALTERNATIVES: You can also use water-soluble stabilizers, which dissolve when submerged in water. Sulky Paper Solvy is a semitransparent paper that you can trace onto or even run through a copy machine or printer. Sulky Solvy (not Ultra Solvy, which is too thick for hand embroidery) is a clear, cellophane-like material. Both tear-away and water-soluble stabilizers work well and have their uses, but I prefer the fabric tear-away stabilizer over the plastic-y material of the Solvy. A drawback of water-soluble stabilizers is that you have to submerge your finished embroidery in water. Tissue paper is a cheap and easy alternative, too. It works much like the tear-away stabilizer but is more fragile. Dampening the tissue paper after stitching makes it a bit easier to remove.

Transfer Paper

Transfer paper is a general-purpose crafting material. It works much like carbon paper or a rubbing to transfer images onto fabric, paper, and even wood and metal. Layer the template (or any image or printout) over a sheet of transfer paper placed facedown over your fabric. Make sure all the layers are securely in place by taping them down to your work surface with painter's tape, so they don't move while you're tracing. Then, with a dull pencil, pen, or tracing stylus, trace over the lines of the template.

I like Loew Cornell and Saral transfer papers, which both come in a variety of colors, are easy to transfer, and are reusable. Do not use a graphite transfer paper, because it is permanent and won't wash out.

WHY YOU MIGHT LOVE IT: Transfer paper is great for transferring patterns onto light or dark fabrics. Just use a light-colored transfer paper for dark fabric and a dark paper for light fabrics. Most transfer papers can be washed out, or even removed by rubbing with your fingers.

WHAT YOU MIGHT NOT LIKE ABOUT IT: Even if you use a tracing stylus to transfer your design, it will leave an impression, like embossing, on your original template, and using a pen or pencil will mark the original. The transfer paper lines are not permanent (which is a good thing), so they can rub off or become less visible as you work, which can be frustrating. It's more difficult to work with this transfer method on soft, stretchy, or coarse fabrics. And since you are marking the template, you can't directly see your fabric. Check periodically to make sure your marks are coming through and lining up right, and that every part of the pattern has been traced and transferred. It's difficult to line up the pattern to the fabric transfer once the template has been removed.

Water-Soluble Pen & Light Box Method

One of the easiest ways to create a pattern is to mark your fabric directly with a water-soluble pen or pencil. This method is best used with a light box or bright window. It's easier to use a light box, but a window works just as well. In either case, tape your template layered under your fabric to the work surface. Trace the lines of the template onto the fabric with a water-soluble pen or pencil. Once you're done stitching, pat the pen or pencil marks with a damp cloth or lightly spray with water to remove.

WHY YOU MIGHT LOVE IT: It's fast and convenient. Your lines are not permanent. You can adjust your stitches without worrying about your lines showing through when you are done stitching, and you can make new marks as you stitch.

WHAT YOU MIGHT NOT LIKE ABOUT IT: Many of these types of pens come in light blue, purple, and pink, which are not good for transferring onto dark fabrics. Try a white pencil or Clover's White Iron Water Soluble Marker for dark fabrics. Keep in mind that the marks (of Clover's White Iron Water Soluble Marker) are not instantly visible—they need to dry before you can see them. The pen or pencil tugs a bit at the fabric, so it may shift the template a bit. Heavy marks can be harder to wash out. I find that heat can make invisible water-soluble pen marks reappear, leaving a ghostly stain, which is super easy to remove with water, but can be a surprise when you're not expecting to see another color on your fabric.

ALTERNATIVES: Bohin Transfer Veil is a thin, transparent material used to duplicate patterns. It is sold in most quilting stores. To use, trace the pattern directly onto the transfer veil with the water-soluble pen that comes with this set. Then, layer the transfer veil over your fabric and retrace. Your marks will bleed through the veil onto light- to medium-colored fabrics, and there is no need for a light box or window. The drawbacks are that the water-soluble pen will mark the original pattern and that you need to trace the pattern twice. You can also use the pattern multiple times and wash the transfer veil to reuse.

Iron-On Transfer Pen

These pens work much like traditional iron-on transfers, but you create the image with your own marks. Simply trace over a printout or image onto paper. Lay the paper face down onto your fabric and iron. Your marks will be in reverse, so for text you'll need to first have a mirror image to trace.

WHY YOU MIGHT LOVE IT: You can trace directly onto any paper and simply iron onto fabric, which simplifies the process of transferring a pattern.

WHAT YOU MIGHT NOT LIKE ABOUT IT: Your pattern is always in reverse. Iron-on transfer pen is permanent, thick like a marker, and often visible on the fabric under your embroidery work. It's not ideal for tweaking a pattern as you stitch.

DIY Printable Fabric Paper

My craft arsenal includes a rather unlikely material, freezer paper. I use it not only to cover my work surface, but to make a temporary fabric stiffener or backing. It's great for creating appliqué fabric shapes and DIY printer paper!

Freezer paper has both a glossy and a matte surface. Iron the matte side of the freezer paper, glossy side face down, onto fabric to create a temporary bond. It's best on smooth, tight- to medium-weave fabrics that don't stretch much. To create your own fabric paper, cut a piece of freezer paper and fabric that is a bit larger than 8½ by 11 in/21.5 by 28 cm. Fuse the two together, concentrating on the corners and edges. Cut the piece down to printer size with a rotary blade and ruler. Iron flat again if the paper is separating, and trim any stray threads. It's important that there are no loose threads that can cause your printer to jam. The freezer paper will easily peel away and leaves no residue.

STITCH DICTIONARY

WHY YOU MIGHT LOVE IT: You can print your own fabric paper, come on! Printing a pattern directly onto your work surface saves you time and opens up lots of creative possibilities. This method works great on light- to medium-colored fabrics.

WHAT YOU MIGHT NOT LIKE ABOUT IT: This method is not great for dark fabrics. Plus, your ink-jet lines are somewhat permanent. I wouldn't wet or wash this fabric, so either cover the lines of the print with your stitches or incorporate the print into your design. And, if your printer is anything like mine, you never know when it will decide not to cooperate. Experiment with it, and hopefully it'll work for you.

For every stitch listed here, there are a gazillion more. There are variations of stitches, composite stitches, and on top of that, each stitch will look different depending on the type of thread you use. But don't worry about becoming a Level Five Stitch Master. Just experiment and see which stitches you like best. With these stitches, you're covered for all the projects in this book, and then some.

There are two types of stitching methods for embroidering—"stab" and "sewing." With the stab method, the needle goes up and down through the fabric, coming up from below, is pulled through, and then it goes down through the fabric. With the sewing method, the needle stays on the top of the fabric. The movement is more side to side, rather than up and down as in the stab method. The sewing method is how most stitches are visualized in embroidery books, but they can be somewhat confusing to piece together and, I find that the stab method provides greater control over the placement of stitches. For this reason, the images and text in the Stitch Dictionary primarily use the stab method with a few exceptions.

Starting and Ending a Length of Thread

The easiest way to start and end a length of thread is by tying a knot. Knots are also the way to go for pieces that will be washed. Back in the day, knots were no-nos for fine needlework. The piece was meant to be just as neat on the back as it was in the front. I'm not going to lie: I use knots all the time. The trick is to tuck the tail ends of the thread under previous stitches, which you can do as you stitch or after a few stitches are made.

To tuck as you stitch, do not make a knot, but as you make your first stitch from below, leave about 1 in/2.5 cm of thread on the back side of your fabric. Be careful not to pull it through. Make the first stitch as you normally would, but for your second stitch make sure the thread on the back goes over the loose thread, locking it down in place. Keep checking on the back side of the fabric as you stitch, until three or four stitches are over the loose thread. You can also manually tuck in the threads: Leave a length of about 3 in/7.5 cm of thread loose on the back side of your piece. Stitch normally, making sure not to pull your thread through. Once about 1 in/2.5 cm of stitches have been made, rethread the loose strand and thread it under stitches a few times, and then snip. I often will start a length of thread with a knot but then end it by tucking the end of the thread under a few stitches and snipping close to the fabric.

For dense, fill stitches, you can tie a knot at the end of a thread length and go down into the fabric from the *top*. With the knot on the front of the fabric, make a few small, straight stitches close together to secure the thread. Then pull up a bit on the knot and snip it off. Stitching over these small stitches with your fill stitch will neatly lock the thread in place.

THREAD LENGTH: Don't fight me on this! I swear it's for your own sanity. Your thread length for stitching should never be more than 24 in/61 cm, ideally about 14 to 18 in/ 35.5 to 46 cm. Any longer and it can strain your arm, cause your threads to get easily tangled, and take you forever to make a single stitch. Besides, when you're stitching, the shine and luster of your thread gets worn away and threads weaken.

WORKING THREAD: This thread is the one on your needle. As you embroider, the working thread will decrease. Tug your needle up along the thread as you stitch.

STANDARD STITCH LENGTH: Stitches should be about 3/16 in/5 mm, but can vary.

Running Stitch

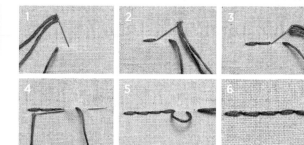

The running stitch is a simple, fast stitch that's good for outlining. Come up through the fabric and down a stitch length, about 1/4 in/6 mm. Come up again through the fabric close to the last hole, and down again. Keep the lengths of the stitches and between the stitches even.

The running stitch is simple to do with the sewing method. Gather a few stitches onto your needle by picking up a few pinches of fabric with your needle point. Come up through the fabric and pull through. Pierce your needle into the fabric about a stitch length away as you also exit the fabric about 1/8 in/ 3 mm away from the original hole. Don't pull the needle through yet. Again, pierce your needle about a stitch length away and gather a couple more stitches onto your needle, just like the first stitch. Now pull through. This will create stitches in a dashed line.

Backstitch

Images 1–3 show the stab method, 4 and 5, the sewing method.

The backstitch is widely used for outlining and text because it creates a smooth, continuous line. Start with a simple forward stitch, coming up through the fabric and then back down through the fabric. Come up through the fabric again about a stitch length ahead of your second hole and then go back down into that second hole. Repeat, trying to keep your stitches uniform in length. Placing your stitches too close together makes for a lumpy, wiggly line.

Threaded Stitch & Whipped Stitch

Both of these stitches are add-ons to previously made stitches that are great for decorative borders or to create bold lines. Theses stitches work best with contrasting colors. The threaded stitch has a loopy, side-to-side appearance, which I call "the snake." The whipped stitch is "the candy cane" because it wraps around the previous stitch, creating bands of color.

> **TIP:** It helps to use the dull end of the needle for these two types of stitches once you've come up through the back of the fabric.

THREADED STITCH

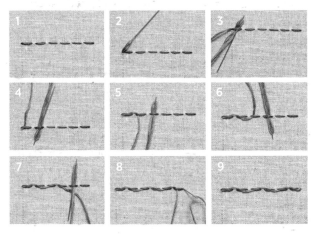

After stitching a segment of running stitches, backstitches, or even chain stitches, use a contrasting color of thread and come up close to or in the original hole of the previous row of stitches. Thread your needle under the previous stitch without picking up any of the fabric or thread of the stitch. Enter the next stitch going under the stitch just like before, but going the opposite direction now. So, if you entered from the right and stitched to the left, now thread the needle under the stitch from left to right. Don't cross over the stitches (that's the whip stitch). Repeat this process.

DOUBLE-THREADED STITCH

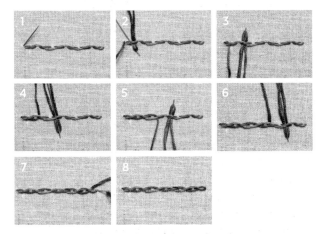

After making a line of threaded stitches, start another row of threaded stitches, but use the opposite route: If your previous stitches were from right to left, left to right, now start left to right, right to left, filling in the pattern as you go.

WHIPPED STITCH

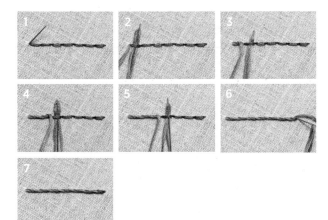

Begin your stitch just as you would with the threaded stitch, but cross over the line of the previous stitches. Once you come up from the back of the fabric, thread the needle under a previous stitch toward the right or left, and always enter the next stitch in that same direction. So, if you enter the stitch on the right, pulling the thread toward the left, your working thread would cross over the previous stitches and enter under the next stitch on the right. Repeat.

Stem Stitch

The stem stitch is used for outlining and can even be used as a fill stitch. It can be worked in a straight line, a curved line, or even on sharp corners. It has a twisted, rope-like appearance that's often used for, well, stems and vines.

Working from left to right, go forward a stitch length, and before pulling though, insert the needle about halfway in between the previous stitch. Now pull through with the working thread either above or below the needle. In either case, be consistent for the following stitches. It's important to hold the working thread always above or below the needle, to achieve the twisted look. Next, go forward a stitch length, and this time insert the needle close to or in the same hole as the previous stitch. Pull through with the working thread in the same position (above or below) your needle. Repeat. To work a corner, come to the end of the line and drop your needle through. Come up close, but not in the same hole, and start a new line of stem stitches. Ideally, the start of the new line will cover the exit point of the previous line.

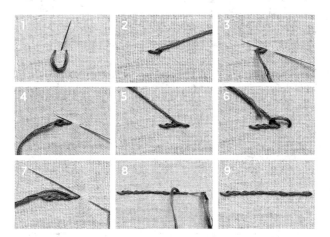

Split Stitch

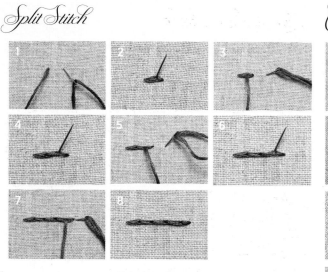

The split stitch is a quick and easy stitch with a fancy braided look. It's great for outlining or filling a space with tightly packed rows. Start with a straight, forward stitch going up through the fabric and then down through the fabric a stitch length away. Come back up through the fabric, piercing the previous stitch in the middle of the stitch, and splitting the plies evenly. Its okay if it's not perfectly in the center of the thread. Pull the thread through. Go forward a stitch length, go down through the fabric, and come up again through that stitch. Repeat.

Chain Stitch

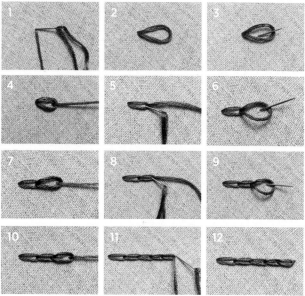

This is my go-to stitch—it's great for outlining, text, and for creating a textured fill. Start by coming up from the back of your fabric. Enter into the same hole you just made, to create a loop. Don't pull the loop through just yet, but leave about ½ in/12.5 mm on top of the fabric. Come up through the fabric about a stitch length away, thread the needle through that loop, and pull the thread through. Again, enter the fabric in the hole you just came up through inside the first looped stitch (it won't pull through, but if you're worried, you can enter close to that hole) and pull until another loop is formed. Enter the fabric a stitch length away and pull through the loop. Repeat.

Detached Chain Stitch & Lazy Daisy Stitch

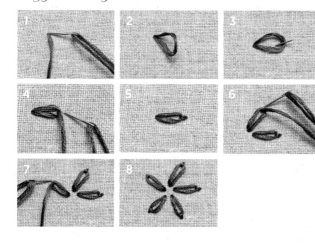

The detached chain stitch, which forms the lazy daisy stitch, is the basis for the chain stitch, so it is worked just like the chain stitch. But instead of continuing lengths of chain, the first loop is anchored to the fabric with a short straight stitch from inside the loop to just outside the loop. This is a detached chain stitch. When this stitch is worked in a circle, like flower petals, it forms the lazy daisy stitch.

Long & Short Stitch

The long and short stitch is another fill stitch that is similar to the satin stitch, but creates texture and is used for shading or gradating colors. You work in sectioned rows that blend into each other. You can be very systematic with it, so that the stitches follow a strict pattern, or more organic with it, which I prefer for a more natural look.

To start the long and short stitch, mark the area to be filled with guidelines, where rows of stitches will come and where you can change colors. Along one edge of the area to be filled, or even from the center out, alternate between longer and shorter straight stitches, staggering the lengths so that some are much smaller, some much longer and some are in between. To create gradated colors, each band should be a new similar color in increasing or decreasing darkness. Blend in the next row of stitches by coming up from the previously stitched holes and again varying the stitch lengths. For an even more seamless blend of graduated colors, come up into the previous stitches, like a split stitch, and just as before, vary the stitch lengths and continue until the shape is filled.

Satin Stitch & Padded Satin Stitch

SATIN STITCH

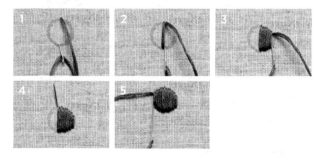

The satin stitch is an easy fill stitch, great for covering larger open areas with a smooth finish. Traditionally, the satin stitch is made with an unstranded thread, for a very smooth finish, but it can be worked with stranded thread as well. If the area is too wide, the stitches can look loose. In that case, you can break up the area into parts and change the direction of the satin stitches. This creates a nice visual effect since the light will look different on the surface of the stitches.

To create a satin stitch, simply come up from the back of your fabric at the center outside edge of the shape to be filled in, jump across with your needle to the opposite center outer edge, and pull the thread through. Pierce your fabric at an angle, as if you are wrapping around your design. Working out toward the edge of the shape, make parallel, straight, closely spaced, but not overlapping, stitches. Now fill in the opposite side of the shape. I work in halves to help keep my work even, because otherwise I might start slanting my satin stitches.

PADDED SATIN STITCH

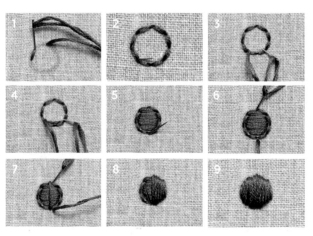

The padded satin stitch creates a raised, more three-dimensional smooth effect. You can do this simply by outlining the shape to be satin stitched with the backstitch. For an even greater padded effect, add straight stitches to fill the area of the shape after the backstitch outline. These fill stitches should run perpendicular to the final satin stitches. Then, add satin stitches, starting in the center and working out. The top satin stitches come around the outside of the filled shape on each outer edge.

Fishbone & Open Fishbone

FISHBONE

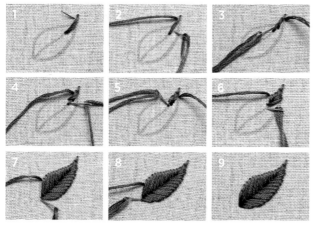

This stitch is a great fill stitch that creates texture and lends itself perfectly to leaf shapes. Start by coming up through your fabric at the tip of your shape, and with your thread create a center line, or spine. You can also just draw this in with a water-soluble pen, but I find it helpful to have the line running along the length of the shape. I find this spine especially useful for curvy leaf shapes. Now, come up along your guide marks, close to the tip, on the right of the previously made spine. Cross over the spine and down a bit, and then go down through the fabric. Repeat this on the left-hand side, coming up close to the tip following the outline of the shape, then crossing over the central spine and your previous stitch, and then going down into the fabric, right where your previous stitch went, but on the opposite side of the spine. This crisscrossing creates a woven look. Keep the stitches close together, without overlapping.

OPEN FISHBONE

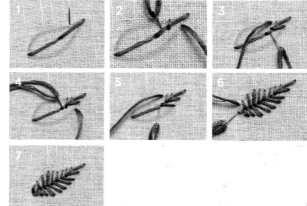

An open fishbone stitch is worked similarly, but instead of filling the space completely, leave spaces between the stitched lines to let the fabric show through. Angle the stitch lengths so that they cover the previous stitch's entry point into the fabric.

Buttonhole Stitch

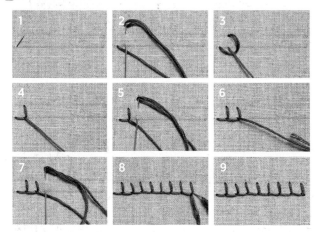

The buttonhole stitch, or blanket stitch, is a decorative stitch that can be worked in many ways—straight, circular, dense, or open. When it's worked on the edge of fabric, it is called the blanket stitch. The stitch is easily worked in the "sewing method." The buttonhole stitch is worked on two parallel lines. It is helpful to draw these two lines, but it is not necessary. Start at the bottom edge or the side that will form the continuous line. Come up through the fabric and pull through. For the next entry point, go down a stitch length (from the bottom line) and upward a stitch length on the parallel line of the stitch. In one motion, pierce this point and the point directly below it on the bottom line with your needle, but don't pull through just yet. Make sure that your working thread is below the needle, and pull through. Repeat.

You can also stagger the lengths upward on the stitch. Hold the working thread taut as you stitch. To finish a row, anchor the last stitch by dropping the thread just outside the last stitch.

Cross & Star Stitch

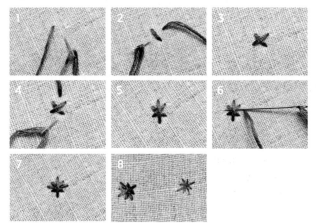

Start out the star stitch with a simple cross-stitch, an "X" shape. You can then make another cross-stitch diagonally to form a star, or stitch in straight single lines to make additional star arms. Vary the lengths of the arms of the cross and the sizes of the stitch itself to give your stars some twinkle. When making a starry sky, varying the sizes of the stars and the number of thread plies helps to create a sense of depth (image 8).

Feather Stitch

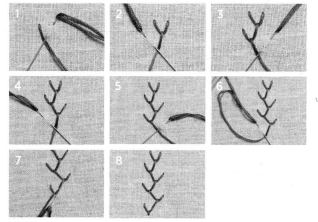

You see this one a lot in crazy quilts, which I love, so I just had to include it in the book. It's a great decorative stitch for borders and goes well paired with French knots.

This stitch works by forming "V" shapes together, both side to side and top to bottom. Sounds complicated, but once you get the rhythm, it's a fun stitch. Start by coming up through the fabric and pulling your thread through. In one motion, enter the fabric a little more than a stitch length to the side of the previous point, and angle the needle (over the thread) to exit the fabric at a point below and in the center of the two previous points, creating a "V" shape. Pull the thread through. Move your needle to the opposite side of the previous stitch, about a stitch length away. In one motion, enter and exit the fabric creating a "V" shape. This time a loop is formed when you exit the fabric. Pull it through

making sure the working thread is below the needle. Work the "V" shapes back and forth, working toward the center of the stitch. To end a feather stitch, anchor the "V" shape with a single straight stitch from inside to outside of the "V" shape.

French Knot

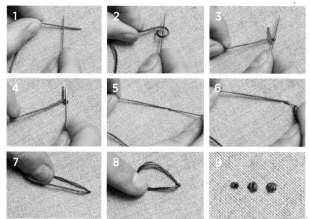

This stitch is all about getting the right tension. To start, it requires two hands, so after you come up through the fabric, place the hoop on a flat surface—your lap or a table. Hold the working thread taut about 1 or 2 in/2.5 or 5 cm from the fabric with your nondominant hand. With your other hand, wrap the thread around the needle once, twice, or even three times for a larger knot (image 9), and keep the tension tight. Now hold the thread taut below the wrapped needle. Insert the needle with your dominant hand back into the fabric close to, but not in, the original hole. Don't pull through yet, but instead, slide the knot down the needle with your nondominant hand to meet the fabric. Keep the tension tight on the working thread being held by your nondominant hand, and begin to lift the hoop up with this hand, so that you are able to pull the needle through the knot. Pull the needle down through the knot and fabric slowly, trying to keep the tension on the thread all the way as you pull through. If you're fighting to pull your needle through, then your tension is too tight. Wiggle your needle a bit and try pulling through again.

Coral Knot

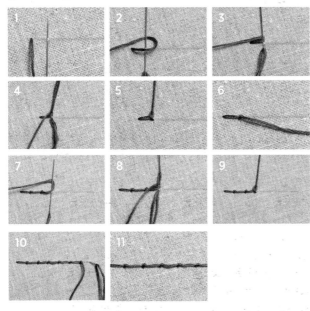

I like the coral knot, or coral stitch, as a simple, decorative border. It's a fast stitch that can be worked in a curve or straight line and combines a straight line with little knots. This stitch is worked in the sewing method.

Come up through the fabric and pull through. Enter and exit a small section of the fabric along the line you're stitching. With the working thread over and then looping under your needle, pull though. The length of the stitch is variable and simply consists of the length between knots. Keep the distance between knots consistent, whether close together or spaced apart.

When working a spaced-out coral stitch, keep the working thread taut, so that the spaces between stitches are not loose.

SIMPLE STITCH SAMPLER

Samplers are needlework pieces combining a variety of stitches and usually featuring decorative borders, scripture verses, simple phrases, and alphabets. They are meant to be elaborate representations of a stitcher's skill, which traditionally was viewed as a sign of virtue. Skilled needlework was once taught to young girls to encourage literacy. I'm often floored when I see a fine sampler and discover that the maker was a young schoolgirl.

This decorative simple sampler is meant to help you jump in and get stitching right away. Each line uses a different stitch. The sampler allows you to learn and practice the stitches used in the book, and the end result is beautiful to boot. Just follow the order of stitches and photo on page 33 to create a sampler of your own.

Materials

9-by-9-in/23-by-23-cm square of fabric

7-inch/17.5-cm embroidery hoop

Embroidery Thread (DMC threads shown: 920/copper, 3814/aquamarine, 3852/yellow)

Size 5 embroidery needle

Scissors

Water-soluble pen (or other transfer medium, optional)

Ruler (optional)

TIME: TAKE YOUR TIME

1 Gather together your basic materials: your fabric, embroidery hoop, thread, embroidery needle, and scissors. Draw the pattern freehand onto your fabric using a water-soluble pen and ruler or transfer the pattern using your favorite transfer method. Either way, the idea of this project is just to give you an opportunity to practice these stitches, so there's no need to stress over perfect lines or perfect stitches.

2 Mount your fabric in your embroidery hoop. Lay the inner hoop onto a sturdy work surface. Place your fabric over the ring and center it. Tighten the hardware of the outer ring so that it just fits over the inner ring. Slide the outer ring over the inner ring, stretching the fabric smooth and taut. Remove any wrinkles by gently tugging on the fabric edges.

3 To start a length of thread, cut the embroidery thread approximately an arm's length (14 to 24 in/ 35.5 to 61 cm), and thread your needle. I used the full six embroidery strands, or plies, of DMC thread for this piece, because I wanted bold, thick lines so you could really see how each line of stitches differs from the next.

4 Working from top to bottom, use the Stitch Dictionary (see page 19) to guide you in the completion of each line of embroidery stitches. Try using alternating colors, especially for the threaded stitches and whipped stitches, so you can see the full effect.

From top to bottom, the stitches used in the sampler are:
Running stitch
Backstitch
Threaded stitch
Whipped stitch
Stem stitch
Split stitch
Chain stitch
Lazy daisy stitch
Long and short stitch
Satin stitch and padded satin stitch
Fishbone stitch
Cross-stitch and star stitch
Buttonhole stitch or blanket stitch
Feather stitch
French knot
Coral knot

5 Frame your finished work in your embroidery hoop (see Finishing Techniques, page 132, for ideas on displaying your work) for a lovely and helpful reference for all your future embroidery projects.

Welcome

HOME & HEARTH

The
Montaño
Family
est. 1948

FAMILY PLAQUE

Where is home for you? For me, I think of my grandparents' little house in Santa Monica. It's sweet oranges straight off the tree in their backyard, cut by my grandma into slices with a knife my grandfather made in his casita, and shared while we lazily swing on the back porch. Wherever home is for you, this family plaque will be a sweet reminder. I made this to give to my grandparents, but like most things I make for others, I just want to keep it for myself. It makes a great gift for a new family, a housewarming, or to celebrate your own family roots. It also works as an anniversary or wedding present.

The pattern can be adapted a few different ways, so there is a lot of flexibility and opportunity to get creative. We'll use Wonder Under, which fuses to fabric and has a tear-away paper backing, to create appliqué pieces. For a super-easy version, you can also use the template as a straight embroidery pattern and forgo the appliqué pieces altogether. You can also try framing the house and smoke in two separate hoops and then hanging the finished pieces a bit staggered, or use this pattern on a throw pillow cover. The appliqué piece will be washable if set correctly.

Materials

Family Plaque Template

Alphabet Template 1

Scissors

Pellon Wonder Under

Extra Fine Point Sharpie

Ruler

Fine-point water-soluble pen

Tracing paper

Pencil (optional)

6-by-6-in/15-by-15-cm light-colored fabric piece for appliqué parts, ironed (muslin and cotton shown)

9-by-9-in/23-by-23-cm fabric piece for background, ironed

Light box (optional)

Iron

Tweezers

7-in/17.5-cm embroidery hoop

Embroidery Thread
(DMC thread shown: 310/black)

Size 7 embroidery needle

Sewing pins (optional)

TIME: 5 TO 7 HOURS

1 Cut out a piece of Wonder Under about 8 by 8 in/ 20 by 20 cm square. Wonder Under has a smooth and a rough side. Place the smooth side face up over the Family Plaque Template and trace the pattern shapes (smoke cloud, text, text guidelines, and house) with a Sharpie, using a ruler to keep the lines straight. The template is reversed, so you'll end up with a mirror image of the template in the final piece.

> NOTE: The words "The," "Family," and "est." have been provided in the template to help minimize your work, but feel free to get creative and use other text. How about your address, name, or even your own free-form text? If you want to use free-form text, simply write your text with a water-soluble pen once your smoke appliqué piece has been fused to the background fabric.

2 Create your customized text. Draw a straight guideline with a ruler and a Sharpie onto a sheet of tracing paper. Place the tracing paper over the alphabet pattern, lining up the bottom of the alphabet letters with the guideline. Trace the letters of your choice with pencil or Sharpie. Try to space the letters evenly and check to make sure the bottom of the letters on the alphabet template meet the guidelines.

3 Transfer the custom text to the Wonder Under. Flip the tracing paper over so that it is backward. Place the Wonder Under pattern over the tracing paper, smooth side up, and trace again with a Sharpie. Line up the straight line you created on the tracing paper with the text guideline and center the text using the central guideline. Trace with a Sharpie.

4 Make the appliqué pieces. You can use different fabrics for the two appliqué shapes (house and smoke). I used a vintage quilt square remnant for the house shape and a natural lightweight cotton for the smoke. Choose fabrics with patterns and textures that don't compete with each other or the background. Iron the wrong side of the fabric for the appliqué pieces to the rough side of the Wonder Under with a hot, dry iron. Press for 5 to 8 seconds, then set aside and let cool.

5 Transfer your text to the fabric. You may be able to see your text pattern on the Wonder Under through a light-colored fabric. If not, use a light box or bright window (tape your appliqué piece securely to the window). Trace (for the very last time, I promise) your text with a fine-point water-soluble pen onto the front of your fabric. Use a ruler to keep the lines of the letters straight. If you'd like to embroider the house details, like the windows and doors, trace these too. You can also cut these parts out later so that the background shows through. No need to trace the outer lines of both shapes, because you will cut these outer lines.

6 Cut the outer edge of the house and the smoke shapes. Cut the windows and the door of the house, or leave these shapes in place to embroider the details.

7 Peel the paper backing from the appliqué pieces and lay the pieces out over your background fabric. Tweezers are helpful if the backing is tricky to remove. You can also try bending the fabric and working at the corners. If you wish to mount your finished embroidery piece in a hoop, use the inner ring of a 7-in/17.5-cm embroidery hoop (or larger, if you wish) to help you arrange the pieces.

8 Once you have the layout you like best, iron the appliqué pieces to the background fabric. The iron should be on a dry (you don't want to wet the water-soluble pen), wool setting. Press the fabric firmly for 10 to 15 seconds or until the fabric is fused.

> **NOTE:** Heavier fabrics will require more time. You can also turn your background fabric over and press from the reverse side as well, to ensure fusion.

9 Mount the background fabric in the embroidery hoop. Embroider the text and any details you'd like for the house. For stitching the text, use a 2- to 4-ply thread for nice, thin letters.

10 You can embellish the appliqué borders with a simple stitch on the edge if you'd like. Try a simple single stitch from the background fabric over the edge of the appliqué piece, as if you were anchoring it down, or use a buttonhole stitch for a hand-embroidered appliqué look.

11 Once your piece is finished, hang it in the embroidery hoop (or see Finishing Techniques, page 132, for more ideas). You can also use this pattern for clothing and home textiles. The appliqué pieces are washable, but I'd sew a line along the edges with a sewing machine if you think you might be washing this piece a lot.

You Are Here

YOU ARE HERE

Close your eyes and imagine your childhood home. Can you navigate the space in your mind? Can you recall the number of steps down the hall? Where are the walls? The doors? This blueprint-inspired project will be a fun memory challenge as you reconstruct a space in your mind and then in needle and thread. It is a great gift for a first-time home buyer, or to memorialize a cherished space.

For this project, I reconstructed my beloved Brooklyn apartment, complete with some furnishing details (and two lazy cats!). If there are multiple stories in the space you'd like to re-create, separate each story into distinct images, one above the other on a single fabric piece or in multiple pieces. It would also be great to add embroidered text noting each room or even locations of momentous occasions within the space.

Materials

Alphabet Template 2 (optional)

Graph paper

Pencil and eraser

Transfer paper

Painter's tape

Fabric, size varies

Ruler

Dull pencil, pen tip, or tracing stylus

Embroidery hoop, size varies

Sulky Stiffy or Pellon Stitch-N-Tear Stabilizer (optional)

Embroidery Thread (DMC thread shown: 3865/white)

Size 5 embroidery needle

iDye Navy (optional)

TIME: 1 HOUR AND MORE, DEPENDING ON THE SIZE OF YOUR PIECE

1 Imagine the space you'd like to embroider. Sketch on graph paper to reconstruct a diagram of the space. Don't worry about being architecturally correct or perfecting the proportions. The graph paper lets you guesstimate proportions well. It's best to start with one room and then base the other rooms on that one for scale.

2 Use your drawing as your pattern or enlarge it if you'd like. It's easy to enlarge your finished floor plan. Just multiply the graph squares by the number of times you'd like to enlarge and redraw onto another sheet of graph paper. For example, if you'd like the drawing to be two times the size of your original and a room is 2 by 4 squares on the graph paper, your new enlarged room would be 4 by 8 squares.

3 Transfer your graph paper pattern onto your fabric. Use the transfer paper method here, especially for dark fabrics. With painter's tape, anchor down your fabric, then on top of it place a sheet of transfer paper (light-colored for dark fabrics, dark-colored for light fabrics), face down, and then place your graph paper pattern on top. Retrace the lines of the graph paper with a ruler and a dull pencil, pen tip, or tracing stylus. Take a peek at your fabric by lifting up a corner of your transfer paper, being careful not to disturb the placement, to make sure your lines are transferring clearly. Retrace any faint lines.

4 Mount your fabric into your embroidery hoop. I used a stabilizer behind my fabric to help create a sturdy surface. I wanted the lines of my piece to be nice and straight like any blueprint would look. Stabilizer is optional, but I find that it helps minimize the stretching of the fabric, which can distort pattern lines.

5 Embroider the lines of your diagram using your favorite stitch. Here's what I did:

OUTLINES: 4-ply split stitch.

INTERIOR DETAILS: 1-ply backstitch.

THE LITTLE CATS: 1-ply satin stitch.

TEXT: 6-ply backstitch.

The final touch is a single cross-stitch, or "x," made at my entryway, where I'll hang the finished piece.

6 The piece is ready to frame now! Mount the piece in your working hoop or in a frame (see Finishing Techniques, page 132).

NOTE ON FABRIC: I tried to find a "blueprint-colored" fabric for this piece. I wanted it to be like a cyanotype with rich navy tones. I couldn't find the right fabric, so I made my own by dyeing light-colored linen fabric with a fabric dye (I used iDye Navy for all-natural fabrics). An indigo dye would work well too.

GOOD LUCK HORSESHOE

I enjoy good old wives' tales and superstitions in general. Over my front door hangs a horseshoe pointing up, to collect any nearby luck of course. Whether you like to wish on stars or throw salt over your shoulder, putting a little horseshoe over a door or bed just might be a welcome invitation for luck. And hopefully it will bless the home and its guests with good fortune.

Add names and a date to this piece, or keep it simple and just embroider the horseshoe. You can also skip the appliqué piece to make a quick, simple gift. This little stitched horseshoe is perfect not only for a housewarming gift, but also as a New Year's or birthday gift.

Materials

Horseshoe Template

Alphabet Template 2

Tracing paper

Pencil and eraser

Extra Fine Point Sharpie

Ruler

Pellon Wonder Under

Iron

5-by-5-in/12.5-by-12.5-cm appliqué piece (optional)

8-by-8-in/20-by-20-cm background fabric piece

Scissors

Transfer method (tear-away stabilizer or water-soluble pen and light box method suggested; see pattern instructions)

Sewing pins (optional)

6-in/15-cm embroidery hoop

Embroidery Thread (DMC threads shown: 731/green, 844/gray, 758/peach, 712/creme)

Size 5 embroidery needle

TIME: 3 TO 5 HOURS (IF YOU SKIP THE APPLIQUÉ AND NAMES: 2 HOURS)

1 Create your pattern. Trace the Horseshoe Template onto a sheet of tracing paper with a pencil, then a Sharpie. If you are not including text, skip to step 4.

2 Customize your pattern. If you are adding text, do not trace the inner circles. First, draw a horizontal line with a ruler above the names (or any text), indicating where they will line up on each side. The first letter should start where your horizontal line touches the text guideline on the right, and the last letter of the text will meet this line on the left.

3 Use the line just inside the horseshoe as the text guideline. Line up the bottom of the alphabet letters with the guideline. Trace the letter of your choice and space the letters apart evenly. On the left, start with the last letter of the text and work backward. Now trace the horseshoe nail holes if there is room. You can fudge the pattern and put them farther or closer to the text if needed.

4 Trace the horseshoe pattern and nail holes only, not the text, onto the smooth side of a small piece of Wonder Under with a Sharpie. If you are not going to use an appliqué piece for the horseshoe, skip ahead to step 8.

5 Iron the rough side of the Wonder Under with a hot, dry iron to the appliqué fabric piece for the horseshoe. Press the Wonder Under for 5 to 8 seconds, then set the piece aside and let it cool.

6 Cut out the horseshoe shape and nail holes with small, sharp fabric scissors. Peel the paper backing off of the Wonder Under.

7 Lay your horseshoe appliqué piece onto your background fabric and arrange as desired. Once you have the layout you like best, iron the appliqué piece to the background fabric. The iron should be on a dry, wool setting and pressed firmly for 10 to 15 seconds or until the fabrics are fused.

NOTE: Heavier fabrics will require more time. You can also turn your background fabric over and press from the reverse side as well, to ensure fusing. Let cool.

8 Transfer your text (and horseshoe pattern, if you skipped the appliqué piece) onto the horseshoe using your favorite transfer technique. I recommend using the tear-away or water-soluble pen and light box method (see Transferring & Personalizing Patterns, page 15). For the tear-away method, trace your template onto the stabilizer material in three small parts: right, bottom, and left side. Pin each section and stitch. If you use the light box method, be careful to line up the text with the text guidelines, because the appliqué may have stretched a bit when it was ironed.

9 Mount your piece in a 6-inch embroidery hoop and stitch! Here's what I did:

HORSESHOE SHAPE: 6-ply split stitch.

TEXT: 4-ply backstitch; 2-ply backstitch for the accent color.

BOX AROUND DATE: 6-ply chain stitch.

NAIL HOLES IN HORSESHOE: 6-ply backstitch.

10 Mount your piece in the working embroidery hoop—it's so easy to hang (see Finishing Techniques, page 132, for more details on framing your piece).

WELCOME BANNER

If it were up to me, all text would have a banner around it. I'm a sucker for that furling ribbon shape, as you can see by flipping through this book. It reminds me of old wood-block prints and vintage embroidery pieces. Your banner can say anything you like, but I've made a "Welcome" and "Hello" template for you to try. Just imagine this piece above a doorway or over a bed!

In this project we use a couple materials unusual in embroidery—wire and fabric stiffener. These materials make for a fun three-dimensional, curvy, furling banner.

Materials

Welcome Banner Template (optional)

Scissors

28-by-5-in/71-by-12.5-cm piece of linen (the thicker the better)

Transfer method (transfer paper or water-soluble pen and light box method suggested; see pattern instructions)

4-in/10-cm embroidery hoop

Embroidery Thread (DMC threads shown: 351/orange, 3819/yellow)

Size 5 embroidery needle

Ruler

Water-soluble pen or dressmaker's chalk

Rotary blade

22-gauge craft wire

Wire cutters

Freezer paper

Thick book or picture frame (1½ to 3 in/4 cm to 7.5 cm thick)

Stiffy Fabric Stiffener

Hammer and picture frame nails

TIME: 3 TO 5 HOURS TO MAKE, AND 1 DAY TO DRY

1 Cut a piece of fabric 28 by 5 in/71 by 12.5 cm. It's important that your fabric be preshrunk and ironed.

2 Photocopy the Welcome Banner Template according to the enlargement instructions (or handwrite your own text), and transfer onto the center of the fabric using transfer paper or a water-soluble pen (see Transferring & Personalizing Patterns, page 15).

3 Mount the fabric piece in the embroidery hoop Stitch your text with a 6-ply double-threaded backstitch or your favorite stitch. Add any embroidered embellishments to the fabric piece. Remember, the banner will curve and obscure some parts of it.

4 Measure the width of the banner, 3 in/7.5 cm, and mark the fabric with a water-soluble pen or dressmaker's chalk along the length of your fabric.

Cut along these lines with a rotary blade and ruler. Make sure your rotary blade is on the side of the ruler opposite of your embroidery work.

5 Create a wire armature for your banner by cutting two 30-in/76-cm lengths of craft wire. Straighten the wire as much as possible.

6 Make a small loop at the end of one length of wire. This loop will be sewn to the back of the fabric. For this step through step eight work from the back with fabric piece face down. Tie a knot at the end of a length of 4-ply thread. Hold your wire loop to the back of the fabric at the corner, about ¼ in/6 mm from the edge. Insert your needle from the back of the fabric, just inside the edge of the wire loop, and make a small straight stitch on the front of the fabric. Reinsert the needle into the fabric just above the wire, outside

the loop. Thread the needle around the wire and the previous knot, and then thread the needle through the loop you just created to lock the wire and thread in place (see images 1 to 4).

7 Space stitches along the wire about ½ in/12 mm apart. For the next stich, insert your needle from the back of the fabric, just below to just above the wire, and make a small straight stitch on the front of the fabric. Your working thread should now be at the back of the fabric (wire side) above the wire. Loop the working thread over and then thread the needle under the wire and your previous stitch. Insert the needle into the loop and under the previous stitch too. Pull tight. Keep the working thread taut as you jump about ½ in/12 mm between stitches. Repeat to the end of the wire (see images 5 to 11).

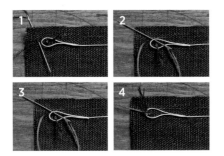

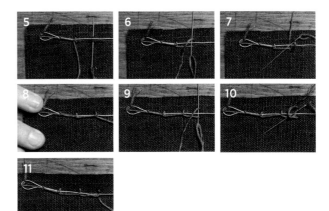

8 At the end of the length of wire, bend the wire to create another loop. Anchor the loop in place as you did for the first loop. You can also tuck your working thread around previous stitches and the wire. Tie a knot in the thread to secure. Repeat this process for the other side of the banner. Don't worry about any frayed edges; we'll cut them toward the end of the project.

9 Cover your work surface with freezer paper, and while you're at it, cover a thick book or picture frame too.

10 Carefully form the banner into a furling ribbon shape with your fingers. Use the covered book or picture frame to help shape the curves of the banner, and give it height. Be careful, because too much messing about can cause the wire to slip out of the stitches. This is easy to fix by coaxing the wire back into shape with your fingers. Leave the banner to rest on the book or frame for the next step.

11 Once you have a shape you like, saturate the fabric with fabric stiffener. You can apply the stiffener directly to the banner and work it into the fabric with your fingers. Make sure to reach any curves and that the fabric is saturated through. Leave the banner to dry completely overnight.

12 Once your banner is dry, trim any loose threads and cut the banner ends to create a banner shape (sideways triangle).

13 To hang the banner, hammer two small picture frame nails into the wall where the banner will touch or come close to the wall. On each side of your banner, where the nails will be, form a bit of wire outward to make two small loops that can rest over the nails.

KEY HOLDER

I come from forgetful stock. I remember my dad coming to me to ask if I had seen his glasses. Why yes, I had—they were on his head! I'm really no better, especially with my keys. The key holder provides a handy, easy way to store keys and is also a welcoming accent to any entryway. It's a clear choice for a housewarming gift, and it makes a great anytime gift for your friends who tend to lose things.

This shadow-boxed embroidery piece can also be a nostalgic display for the house keys to a past home, apartment, or special place. If I ever move, I'll hang my current house keys in it for safekeeping and memories.

Materials

Key Holder Template

Alphabet Template 3

Tracing paper

Pencil and eraser

Extra Fine Point Sharpie

Ruler

7-by-7-in/17.5-by-17.5-cm fabric piece, ironed

Transfer paper or tear-away stabilizer

Water-soluble pen (optional)

Painter's tape

6-in/15-cm embroidery hoop

Sulky Stiffy Stabilizer or Pellon Stitch-N-Tear (optional)

Embroidery Thread
(DMC threads shown: 844/gray, 3809/blue)

Size 7 embroidery needle

Iron

5-by-5-in/12.5-by-12.5-cm picture mat

Shadow-box frame, 5 by 5 in/12.5 by 12.5 cm or larger (perhaps use IKEA Ribba frame, 10 by 10 in/25 by 25 cm)

One ¼-in/6-mm hook

Drill

1/16-in/1.5-mm drill bit

Scissors

Thin board

Linen tape

TIME: 6 TO 8 HOURS

1 First, create your custom template. Trace the Key Holder Template onto tracing paper with a pencil or Sharpie and ruler. Don't forget to trace the text guidelines, two horizontal and one central line, to help you line up your text. Place the tracing paper over the alphabet template, lining up the bottom of the desired letters and numbers with the text guideline. Trace the letters and numbers with a pencil or Sharpie. Try to space the numbers evenly, about ¼ in/6 mm apart. Check to make sure the bottom of the letters on the alphabet template meet the straight text guidelines on the tracing paper. Use the vertical line to center your text.

2 Transfer the pattern onto your fabric piece using your favorite transfer method. (See Transferring & Personlizing Patterns, page 15), for more information on transferring patterns.) For this pattern, I suggest using the transfer paper or water-soluble pen and light box method. Use painter's tape to secure template and fabric to your work surface when transferring the pattern.

3 Mount your fabric into your embroidery hoop. For this project, I used a stabilizer behind my fabric to help create a sturdy surface for the satin-stitched key.

4 Stitch your piece! Here's what I did:

KEY: 6-ply padded satin stitch, outlined first in a 6-ply backstitch. The tricky part is stitching around the three circles at the top of the key. Work in sections starting at the widest part, then the center, and then the sides of the key. Then fill in any holes in the stitching.

ADDRESS: 4-ply backstitch. To create added thickness in the wider parts of the text, I added another row of backstitches. Blend these rows together by entering a previous stitch where the text begins to widen instead of creating a new entry/exit point.

5 Remove the finished embroidery piece from the hoop. Iron the piece smooth on the edges of the fabric to eliminate any hoop marks. Avoid ironing the embroidery. Set aside.

6 Put the hook in your shadow box frame. Make sure that the screw part of the hook will not extend beyond the top of your frame. Measure to find the center point of the top, inside of the frame, and make a pencil mark. With an electric drill, drill a 1/4-in/6-mm-deep starting point with a 1/16-in/1.5-mm drill bit. Then hand-screw the hook into the frame. Make sure the hook faces forward. If it doesn't, remove the hook and reposition it until the hook faces forward.

7 Stretch your fabric around a thin but stiff piece of board that fits into your frame. Secure the fabric in place with linen tape along each side. Place the mat in front of the stretched fabric, secure in place with linen tape, and close the frame back. Now you're ready to hang your finished piece.

ENGAGEMENT

ASN & MAC

2012

July 25, 2009

Toni &

Alex

WEDDING & ANNIVERSARY

CROSSED ARROWS & BANNER

There's a Mexican game of chance called Loteria, which is a lot like Bingo, but instead of numbered pieces the game uses cards with iconic illustrations, great colors, and Spanish text. One of my favorite cards, "Las Jaras," pictures two crossed arrows tied with ribbon. I've always collected these cards and when I see this one I imagine the arrows as people, or lives, tied together forever. What better way to symbolize an engagement, the union of marriage, or an anniversary? The arrows are fierce emblems of the promises we make, friendship, and love.

The three banner text lines can be used to say anything you like—names, a date, or even a location. Use the alphabet template or your own handwritten text to personalize the piece.

Materials

Crossed Arrows & Banner Template

Alphabet Template 3

Tracing paper

Pencil and eraser

Ruler

Extra Fine Point Sharpie

Transfer method (tear-away stabilizer, transfer paper, or water-soluble pen and light box method suggested; see pattern instructions)

Painter's tape

Scissors

10-by-10-in/25-by-25-cm (framed in hoop) or 12-by-12-in/30.5-by-30.5-cm (art board/canvas) fabric piece for background

8-in/20-cm embroidery hoop

Sewing pins (optional)

Embroidery Thread (DMC threads shown: 350/orange red, 504/light green, 992/dark mint green, 3819/green yellow, 3821/yellow, 3853/orange, 3866/cream)

Size 5 embroidery needle

Tweezers (optional)

8-by-8-in/20-by-20-cm frame or canvas for framing (optional)

TIME: 7 TO 9 HOURS

1 Create your customized pattern using both the Crossed Arrows & Banner Template and the Alphabet Template 3. You can also handwrite your text. Using tracing paper, outline the shapes of the template using a pencil and a ruler for the straight lines. Don't forget to trace the gray text guidelines, which will help you arrange your text. There are two rows of guidelines (the upper row is for letters like "j," "p," and "y" that loop down). Place the tracing paper over the alphabet template, lining up the bottom of the alphabet letters with the guideline. Trace the letters of your choice with a pencil or Sharpie. Try to space the letters evenly.

2 Transfer the pattern onto your fabric piece using your favorite transfer method. (See Transferring & Personalizing Patterns, page 15, for more information on transferring patterns.) For this pattern, I suggest using the tear-away stabilizer, transfer paper, or water-soluble pen and light box method. Use painter's tape to secure template and fabric to your work surface when transferring the pattern.

3 Mount your fabric piece in your embroidery hoop. If you used tear-away stabilizer, pin the material to the fabric. Stitch the elements of the pattern in any order you'd like. Here's what I did:

BANNER: 6-ply split stitch with 2-ply backstitch details (shadows on banner curves). The stitch lines don't need to be perfectly straight. In fact, I tried to create an uneven edge by placing my needle inside and outside the pattern line for a feeling of a banner blowing in the wind.

TEXT: 3-ply backstitch.

ARROWS: 6-ply split stitch for the feathers and 6-ply chain stitch for the shafts. The arrows are super fun to stitch. Get creative with the colors you choose for the feathers. Since the arrows are partly obstructed by the banner, you can just jump with your thread to pick up the line and start a new line of chain stitches to complete the arrows.

ARROWHEADS: 6-ply satin stitch worked from the center of the shape out.

4 If you used tear-away stabilizer, remove the material now, slowly and carefully. Using tweezers will help. The trickiest part is removing the material under the satin stitches. I use the dull end of a needle to sweep under longer satin stitches to pick out any excess tear-away material. If you used a water-soluble pen, lightly spray the piece with water or use a damp cloth to remove any visible marks.

5 Mount the piece either by keeping it in the embroidery hoop, or stretching and framing it (see Finishing Techniques, page 132).

TREE RING SAMPLER

"time is a tree (this life one leaf)"
—*e.e. cummings, "as freedom is a breakfastfood"*

The rustic tree rings in this sampler signify not just the passing of time but also growth. Feel free to add more rings or remove some to get the tree rings just right for you. The pattern is a symbolic reminder of familial love, with each ring symbolizing another year together.

Materials

Tree Ring Sampler Template

Alphabet Template 1

Tracing paper

Pencil and eraser

Ruler

Extra Fine Point Sharpie

Transfer method (transfer paper, water-soluble pen and light box, or tear-away stabilizer method suggested; see pattern instructions)

Scissors

7-by-7-in/17.5-by-17.5-cm *or* 8-by-8-in/20-by-20-cm fabric piece, ironed

5-in/12.5-cm *or* 6-in/15-cm embroidery hoop

Embroidery Thread (DMC threads shown: 300/red brown, 838/dark brown, 904/lighter green, 3345/hunter green, 3371/black brown)

Size 5 embroidery needle

Sewing pins (optional)

Tweezers

TIME: 4 TO 5 HOURS

1 Create your customized text. Create your customized pattern using both the Tree Ring Sampler Template and Alphabet Template 1. With a sheet of tracing paper, trace the pattern shapes and gray text guidelines.

2 Place your tracing paper over the alphabet template and line up the bottom of your desired letters to the text guidelines and trace. Using a ruler really helps keep the lines of the letters straight. Keep the spacing of the letters uniform, about 1/8 in/3 mm between the letters.

3 Once you have the pattern traced completely, you can transfer your pattern using your favorite transfer technique (see Transferring & Personalizing Patterns page 15). Using either the transfer paper, water-soluble pen, or the tear-away method will work well for this project.

4 Mount the fabric piece in the embroidery hoop, and start stitching, using the stitch guide below. Pin tear-away stabilizer to your fabric if using this method. Since the leaves are meant to rest on top of the tree rings, it's best to stitch these first. Then stitch the tree rings into, or "under," the leaves. Here's what I did:

LEAF SHAPES: 6-ply fishbone stitch in two forest green tones.

LEAF OVERLAP: The leaf that is overlapped by the other starts in a fishbone stitch, but transitions into a satin stitch. Just keep following the outside guideline and working the stitch at an angle until you reach the end of the shape.

OUTERMOST TREE RING: 6-ply chunky chain stitch. I started at the double leaf shape, coming up as close as possible to the shape. Then I worked around the ring. Then stitch the inner of the two rings. Fill any open spaces between the two rings with another row of chain stitches. If the space is too tight for another row but you see some fabric showing through, just add a few backstitches in those spots.

TEXT AND TREE RINGS: 3-ply backstitch. Keep the lines of the tree rings loose and organic. Feel free to get wiggly with your lines and vary the length of your stitches to help create a natural looking tree. Stitch the text by following the guidelines closely and minimizing stitches (by using longer stitch lengths) for straight, smooth lines. I find the tighter the stitch lengths, the bumpier the text can look.

5 If you used tear-away stabilizer, remove the material now, slowly and carefully. Using tweezers will help. The trickiest part to remove will be under the leaves. Use the dull end of a needle to sweep under the stitches and pull up excess tear-away fabric. If you used a water-soluble pen, lightly spray the visible marks or use a damp cloth to remove them.

6 The shape of this piece is perfect for mounting in an embroidery hoop. To secure the piece to the embroidery hoop, cut off the excess fabric from the outside edge of the piece, leaving a ½-in/12-mm fabric allowance, and cut away all stabilizer material. Glue the fabric allowance to hoop at the back. Your piece is ready to hang. (For more ideas, see Finishing Techniques, page 132.)

WEDDING TABLE MARKERS

Imagine a group of family and friends crafting together to make these simple, elegant table markers. This small, handmade detail will really impress your wedding guests and add warmth and charm to that special day. The project is fun, easy, looks stellar, and can be made in a weekend, or less if you work with your bridal (embroidery) team. These table markers can also be given as gifts after a wedding or used to decorate throughout the year.

I've presented the markers in four different ways (see photo, page 64) to give you some ideas. You can choose the format that best fits your needs or even mix and match. Enlarge the pattern as much as you would like. Just remember to keep it simple and they will look lovely.

Materials

Wedding Table Marker Template

Scissors

Fabric, sizes of pieces vary (see instructions)

Mason jars or birch logs (optional)

3-in/7.5-cm embroidery hoop (for mounting)

Frame (optional, 5 by 7 in/12.5 by 17.5 cm shown)

Water-soluble pen (recommended)

Painter's tape

Transfer paper (optional)

Tracing paper (optional)

Pencil or Sharpie (optional)

4-in/10-cm embroidery hoop (for stitching)

Embroidery Thread (DMC threads shown: 3865/white, 3820/yellow, 937/green)

Size 5 embroidery needle

Iron

Rotary blade

Ruler

Fray Check

Sewing machine (optional)

Sewing pins

Thin board for frame (optional)

Linen tape for frame (optional)

TIME: 20 TO 40 MINUTES PER MARKER

1 Choose how you'd like to display your table markers and cut fabric to appropriate sizes. Cut one piece of fabric per table number desired. For now, make rough cuts with fabric scissors. We'll make more precise cuts later. For the display methods, the sizes of the fabric pieces are:

MASON JAR AND BIRCH LOGS: L (circumference of object + 1 in/2.5 cm) x W (5 in/12.5 cm, but can vary according to your chosen object).

EMBROIDERY HOOP, 3 IN/7.5 CM: 5-by-5 in/12.5-by-12.5-cm.

FRAME: add 1 in/2.5 cm to the length and to the width of the frame's dimensions.

2 Create your number patterns and transfer them onto your fabric using your preferred transfer method (see Transferring & Personalizing Patterns, page 15). Use the water-soluble pen method to save some time. Tape your fabric and template to a light box or sunny window with painter's tape and trace the numbers onto your fabric with a water-soluble pen. Transfer paper works well too, but first make a tracing paper copy or other kind of copy of the template, so that you can make multiple transfers.

3 Mount the fabric in the 4-in/10-cm embroidery hoop for stitching. For the longer strips of fabric, the number should be in the center of the piece. Here's how I stitched the numbers:

NUMBER 1: 6-ply chain stitch, and a simple long backstitch outlining the chain stitch to add a bit more contrast and help the number pop off the floral background fabric.

NUMBERS 2 AND 4: 6-ply whipped backstitch in two contrasting colors.

NUMBER 3: 6-ply chain stitch.

4 Remove the piece from the hoop and iron smooth any hoop marks on the fabric. Avoid ironing the embroidery. (You don't need to iron the fabric if it is going to be mounted in a 3-in/7.5 cm hoop.)

5 Finish your table marker depending on your method of display:

MASON JAR OR A TREE LOG: Measure the desired width of the final fabric piece with a ruler and mark with a water-soluble pen. Cut excess fabric with a rotary blade and ruler. Make sure that the blade is on the side of the ruler opposite your embroidery work, just in case. Seal the fabric edges with Fray Check to prevent the fabric from unraveling. If you'd like a more finished look, you can sew a straight line along the length of both edges of the fabric piece with a sewing machine. Pin the fabric piece around the jar or log, and remove from object. Stitch edges together with a simple backstitch or sew with a sewing machine.

EMBROIDERY HOOP: Cut off the excess fabric from the outside edge of the hooped piece, leaving a ½-in/12-mm fabric allowance. Glue the fabric allowance to the hoop at the back.

FRAME: Stretch your fabric around a thin but stiff piece of board that fits into your frame. Secure the fabric in place with linen tape along each side. Place the mat in front of the stretched fabric on board and close the frame back.

FLOWER BOUQUET

For adding "something handmade" to the wedding mix, this project is perfect. The embroidered piece can be used to commemorate your beautiful wedding day bouquet and can be made in any wedding color scheme. You can also add some text, a date, or even names using your own handwriting or an alphabet pattern from this book.

The pattern template features some of the most popular wedding flowers—calla lily, rose, lily, tulip, orchid, lily of the valley, and some foliage. You are the artist here—create your own perfect arrangement.

Materials

Embroidered Flower Bouquet Template

Embroidery hoop, size varies (6 in/15 cm shown)

Tracing paper

Extra Fine Point Sharpie

Pencil and eraser

Scissors

Transfer method (transfer paper or water-soluble pen and light box method suggested; see pattern instructions)

Fabric piece (varies, depending on hoop size. Add 2 in/5 cm to diameter of hoop to get the width and length of your fabric piece)

Painter's tape

Stabilizer (optional)

Embroidery Thread (DMC threads shown: 305, 580, 890, 3345/greens; 727, 729, 832, 3822/yellows; 720/orange; 154, 814, 3685, 3802/purples; 221, 304/reds; 819/pink; 712/cream)

Size 5 embroidery needle

TIME: VARIES DEPENDING ON YOUR DESIGN. THIS 6-IN/15-CM PIECE FEATURED TOOK 12 TO 15 HOURS. KEEP IN MIND I FILLED IN MY SHAPES WITH DENSE FILL STITCHES, WHICH TAKES MORE TIME.

1 Decide how big you'd like the bouquet to be and what size embroidery hoop you'll need. Place the inner ring of your embroidery hoop onto a sheet of tracing paper and outline the inner diameter with a Sharpie. This circle will be your pattern border.

2 Layer the tracing paper with the border circle over the Embroidered Flower Bouquet Template. Move the tracing paper around over the template, so you can see different possibilities for flower arrangement. Lightly sketch the placement of a few flowers with pencil to see if you like that arrangement.

Create depth by layering the flowers over one another, obscuring parts of some flowers. Use the foliage to come up and around the flowers if you wish to add texture and dimension.

> **TIP:** To change whether a shape is facing left or right, just flip your tracing paper over and trace on the back side of the tracing paper. When you flip it back over, you'll see your marks in reverse.

3 Consider adding any text now, maybe a date around the bottom of the bouquet. Once you have a design you like, trace over your pencil lines with a Sharpie. Erase your pencil marks for a clear pattern to transfer.

4 Using your favorite transfer method (see Transferring & Personalizing Patterns, page 15), transfer the pattern on the tracing paper to the center of your fabric piece. The transfer paper and water-soluble pen methods work best for this project. Use painter's tape to secure both your pattern and fabric before marking the fabric.

5 Mount your fabric into your embroidery hoop. Use stabilizer for added stiffness if you wish.

6 Start stitching! Since the shapes of the flowers are open and have wide spaces to fill, I suggest using fill stitches—satin stitch and long and short stitch. The long and short stitch is great for shading too. You can also keep it simple and outline the shape of the flowers with the chain stitch, split stitch, or backstitch, and then add details into them—small, straight stitches to create lines of movement or texture, French knots for the center details, and stem stitches for the flower stems.

7 Once you are finished embroidering, frame your work within an embroidery hoop, or however you like (see Finishing Techniques, page 132, for more details on finishing your work).

ME & YOU

Oh, that ampersand! It's the bit of typography that joins me and you, that makes "us" and "we" out of two separate people. Everything about this project is a bold declaration of love. The strong lines of the letters, the colors that pop, and the big ol' ampersand connecting it all. It's also a lot of fun to stitch up. Pick bright, contrasting colors for this piece. It looks great mounted in an oval hoop frame.

Materials

Me & You Template

Alphabet Template 4

Tracing paper

Pencil and eraser

Extra Fine Point Sharpie

Ruler

Transfer method (tear-away stabilizer suggested; see pattern instructions)

7-by-12-in/17.5-by-30.5-cm fabric piece, ironed

Scissors

5-by-9 in/12.5-by-23-cm embroidery hoop

8-in/20-cm embroidery hoop (optional)

Sulky Stiffy or Pellon Stitch-N-Tear Stabilizer

Sewing pins (optional)

Embroidery Thread (DMC threads shown: 224/pink, 3822/yellow, 3847/teal, 3865/white)

Size 5 embroidery needle

Tweezers (optional)

TIME: 5 TO 6 HOURS

1 Create your customized pattern. Use a sheet of tracing paper and trace the Me & You Template including the gray text guidelines. Then layer your tracing paper template over the Alphabet Template, line up the bottom of your desired letters to the guideline, and trace the outline of the letters with a Sharpie and ruler.

   TIP: You can forgo making a tracing paper pattern and create one directly onto tear-away stabilizer. This method is great for transferring patterns onto dark fabric, which is what I used for this project.

2 Copy the template according to the enlargement instructions. Transfer the pattern to the fabric using your favorite transfer technique (see Transferring & Personalizing Patterns, page 15).

3 Mount the fabric in the embroidery hoop. I find that oval hoops don't hold fabric as taut as circular hoops do. Using a stabilizer (Sulky Stiffy or Pellon Stitch-N-Tear under the fabric) helps, or you can use an 8-in/20-cm embroidery hoop for stitching, and

then frame the piece in an oval hoop. If you are using tear-away stabilizer, pin your template sheet to the hooped fabric.

4 Start stitching (see Split Stitch, page 24). Here's how I did it and in the order I worked:

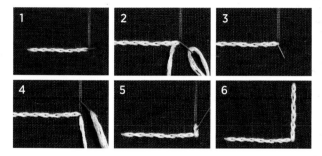

LETTER OUTLINES: 6-ply split stitch. When the letters end in a right angle, the last stitch in that line will not be "split" since you're moving to the new line. But I still "split" this stitch, coming through it in the center and then back in the same exit point from the previous stitch. This makes it look like a completed stitch. I start my next row of stitches going forward a stitch length underneath the fabric, coming up through the fabric, and back into that same hole (basically, a backstitch) along the perpendicular line, and then starting a new row of split stitches.

AMPERSAND OUTLINE: 3-ply split stitch.

NOTE: Stitching curves can be a bit tricky. When you're stitching a curve, shorten your stitch lengths—the tighter the curve, the smaller the stitch. You really notice this with the ampersand.

AMPERSAND DETAILS: wee 3-ply satin stitches.

LEAVES: 4-ply satin stitch.

FLOWER CENTER: 6-ply padded satin stitch. Padding the stitch adds dimension and smooths the shape out better than a singe layer of satin stitches.

FLOWER PETALS: clusters of three 6-ply French knots. I grouped them in a tight triangle shape to help them lie next to one another and to avoid overlapping stitches.

5 If you used tear-away stabilizer, remove the material now, slowly and carefully. Using tweezers will help lots. The trickiest part to remove will be under the satin stitches. I use the dull end of my needle to sweep under longer satin stitches and pull up excess tear-away fabric. If you used the water-soluble pen, lightly spray visible marks or use a damp cloth to remove them.

6 Display your piece either by leaving it in the 8-in/20-cm hoop or transferring it to an oval hoop (see Finishing Techniques, page 132). Your piece is ready to hang!

BABIES & LITTLE ONES

hank

SEA HORSE A Fish In Armor

Best in Children's Books

GOODNIGHT MOON   HARPERCOLLINS

FAIRY TALES OF THE BROTHERS GRIMM   VIKING

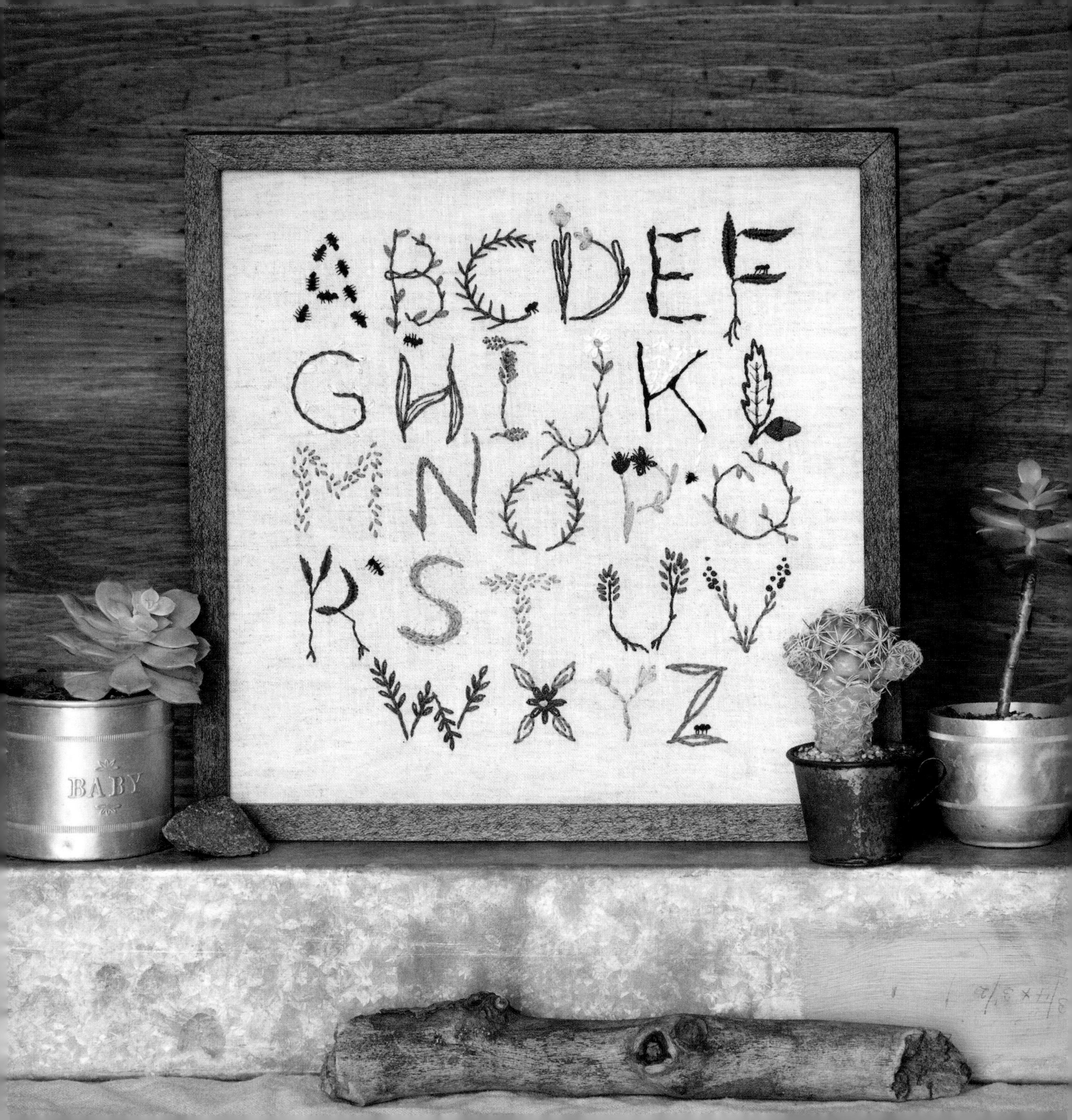
ABCDEF
GHIJKL
MNOPQ
RSTUV
WXYZ
BABY

NURSERY ALPHABET

When I was small, I remember how big the backyard seemed and what a fantastical place it was. The hedges were a labyrinth, the tall trees formed a jungle canopy, and the dirt was my playground. I would dig with sticks, turn stones, and collect feathers, leaves, and roly-polies in paper cups. Kids love exploring the outdoors, and I hope this embroidered piece can bring some of the wonder of nature to you and your little one.

I stitched each letter a bit differently, letting the inspiration of each shape guide my color and stitch choices. There are no rules, just pull out all your threads—that's what I did—and see where you end up!

Materials

Nursery Alphabet Template

12-by-12-in/30.5-by-30.5-cm fabric piece, preshrunk and ironed

Transfer method (DIY printable fabric paper suggested: freezer paper or Wonder Under, or tear-away stabilizer; see step 1 of pattern instructions)

Transfer paper or water-soluble pen (optional)

4-in/10-cm embroidery hoop

9-in/23-cm embroidery hoop

Scissors

Embroidery Thread (assorted DMC colors shown)

Size 7 embroidery needle

Iron

Frame (shown: 10 by 10 in/25 by 25 cm)

TIME: ABOUT 10 HOURS

1 Transfer the pattern onto your fabric. Since this piece has a lot of small details and individual pieces, I experimented with printing directly onto my fabric using the DIY printable fabric paper method (see instructions, page 18–19). If you do print this template directly onto your fabric, decrease the size of the pattern to about 6 by 6 in/15 by 15 cm, so that you can easily hoop your piece. I printed my template onto a sheet of DIY fabric paper, but instead of fabric I used a sheet of tear-away stabilizer, because I wanted to stitch the pattern at the original, larger size. The transfer paper or water-soluble pen methods will also work great here; it just takes a little more time to transfer the pattern.

2 Because the 8-by-8-in/20-by-20-cm image is large, you will want to work in sections with the 4-in/10-cm hoop to stitch your piece. For a 6-by-6-in/15-by-15-cm piece, you can use the 9-in/23-cm hoop. To avoid getting hoop marks on your fabric, remove the piece from the hoop when you are not working on it. Mount the fabric in the hoop at the upper-left corner of the pattern. If you are working with printed tear-away stabilizer, check to make sure that there is enough room on the fabric for the full pattern to be stitched onto it.

3 Begin stitching the letters in the first section. I used a variety of stitches in 3- and 4-ply thread for thin lines. But, if you're using a printed fabric template, use thread that will cover the width of the printed lines. For the first letter, A, use French knots to create little ants. French knots form the bodies, and 1-ply short, straight stitches form the tiny legs.

4 Once the letters in one section are stitched, move on to another section. Be careful when hooping the piece over a previously stitched area. You want to put as little strain as possible on previous stitches and minimize the amount of hooping done over previous stitches.

5 Once you've finished embroidering all the alphabet letters, consider adding little French knot ants throughout the piece to reference that first letter A. Add some of your own details too!

6 Iron any hoop marks smooth. This can be tricky because there are lots of nooks and crannies in this piece. Try ironing the piece face down under a clean, damp cloth. I still had marks on my fabric, so I had to iron the front of the piece too. Try to avoid ironing your stitches as much as possible, and use the tip of the iron to smooth the fabric. (If you stretch your finished embroidery on a frame or art panel, wrinkles and hoop marks will be minimized.)

7 The square shape of this pattern lends itself well to framing or stretching over a canvas (see Finishing Techniques, page 132).

BABY MINE MOBILE

"I love you to the moon and back."
—from *Guess How Much I Love You,* by Sam McBratney

I've got a collection of children's books and every now and then I pull out a few and pore over their pages. They make me smile, inspire me, and—I've just noticed–they are often filled with starry skies. This mobile is a sweet addition to any nursery or baby's room, and shows how you love 'em to the moon and back. Snuggle up together and read a few books under the stars.

You can simplify the project in a few ways, which I walk you through in the instructions. Since the back of the piece will be visible, consider covering the back with fabric and adding some appliquéd or embroidered stars. (See Finishing Techniques, page 132, for more on backing your embroidery.)

Materials

Baby Mine Mobile Template

Transfer method (transfer paper or water-soluble pen and light box method suggested; see pattern instructions)

7-by-7-in/17.5-by-17.5-cm fabric piece, ironed (for embroidery)

5-in/12.5-cm embroidery hoop

Pellon Stitch-N-Tear or Sulky Stiffy stabilizer (optional)

Embroidery Thread (DMC threads shown: 726/dark yellow, 727 light yellow, 445/lightest yellow, 746/off white)

Size 5 embroidery needle

Scissors

Fabric glue

6-by-6-in/15-by-15-cm backing fabric (to cover the back of the embroidery, optional)

Ribbon (optional)

Clipboard

Painter's tape

Wonder Under or glue gun

Extra Fine Point Sharpie

Ruler

Iron

8-by-8-in/20-by-20-cm fabric piece, ironed (for mobile parts)

Tweezers

Electric drill

3/32 drill bit

Pencil and eraser

Tapestry needle

TIME: 3 TO 4 HOURS TO STITCH, PLUS 2 TO 3 HOURS TO ASSEMBLE THE MOBILE

1 Use the template to transfer your pattern. Use transfer paper for this project, which is great for dark fabrics. If you're using a lighter fabric, the light box method would be a good choice (see Transferring & Personalizing Patterns, page 15).

2 Mount your fabric into your embroidery hoop. Use stabilizer for added stiffness if you wish.

3 Using a gradated color scheme, blend the colors with a long and short 4-ply stitch. In very thin areas, the stitch becomes a backstitch. To blend the colors, I drew a horizontal line through the center of the letters on my pattern and used this to eyeball where the two colors should meet. I also blended the colors at the center where the colors meet by varying the long and short stitches. (Some stitches go over and beyond the center line, and some don't quite meet the center line, so the colors weave together nicely.)

4 Once stitching is complete, frame your embroidery piece in the hoop (see Finishing Techniques, page 132). You'll need scissors, fabric glue, and, if you like, fabric to back the piece.

5 Now, make the braided cords from which the mobile parts will hang. If you want to simplify the mobile, skip the braided cords and use ribbon. To make the braided cords, take three colors of embroidery thread and cut eight 12-in/30.5-cm lengths of each color. Separate the threads into eight groups, which include one thread of each color. Knot the ends of the groups. Use a clipboard to hold down the thread as you braid the threads, and then secure the ends of the braids with a small piece of painter's tape.

6 Now we'll make the mobile parts. You'll need two of each piece, one is a mirror reflection, because each mobile part has two sides. We'll sandwich the braided cords between the two sides of each part and secure in place with Wonder Under. I like to use Wonder Under to glue these pieces together because it provides crisp, clean edges to the fabric pieces, but a glue gun or fabric glue will also work well.

Trace the outlines of the mobile shapes onto the smooth side of the Wonder Under using a fine tipped Sharpie and a ruler. Number each shape on the Wonder Under so it will be easy to match up the shapes before removing this layer.

7 On a hot, dry setting, iron the rough side of the Wonder Under to the wrong side of the fabric for the mobile parts. Press the Wonder Under for 5 to 8 seconds. Then let the piece cool for a few minutes. Cut the shapes out and keep them grouped with their matching numbered pair. Peel the paper backing off the Wonder Under, using tweezers to help separate the paper from the fabric. If you are finding it difficult to remove, press for a few more seconds and try again. The paper backing should come off cleanly from the fabric leaving a shiny, smooth surface.

8 Once all the paper backing has been removed from all mobile parts and the pairs are lined up, grab those braided cords. Cut the knot off the top of one cord and lay that end over the back of one mobile piece. Sandwich the other side of the pair over the cord and line up the two mobile pieces. Iron the mobile piece for 10 to 15 seconds or until the two fabrics are fused to lock the cord in place. Trim any stray fabric threads on the mobile piece with scissors if necessary. Repeat for the remaining mobile pieces.

9 Power tool time. Using an electric drill and the 3/32 drill bit, drill 8 holes into the bottom half of your framed embroidery hoop. I staggered the holes a bit, but in general they are about ¾ in/2 cm apart, starting from the center out. First mark the holes on the center width of the hoop with a pencil. Of course, take full care when using the drill. Start the drill slowly so that it doesn't jump around. You won't need too much pressure to make the holes, since the wood is soft and not too thick. I held the hoop straight up and drilled straight down. You can also just glue the braided cords to the back of the hoop (using a glue gun or fabric glue) if you prefer.

10 Remove the painter's tape from the ends of the braided cords. Thread the braided cords onto a tapestry needle and thread through the drilled holes in your hoop. Arrange the cords at various lengths, double-knot the cords inside the back of the hoop, and cut off any excess thread.

Whodathunkit? Power tools and embroidery. Good job!

CHILD'S DRAWING

When I visit home, I find that my little cousins aren't so little anymore. I created this project as a way to keep them small and close. It's a collaboration of handiwork: the child's original artwork and your stitches. For this project you'll be working from your own source materials to create a one-of-a-kind personalized pattern. Try involving kids in the process—have them pick out their favorite drawing, make a special one just for this project, or even have them make some stitches. The backstitch is the ultimate kid-friendly stitch. (For little hands, try a tapestry needle, which has a large eye for easy threading and a blunt point.) You can even stitch onto an iron-on transfer, no pattern-making required!

Materials

Original artwork (drawing, photograph, or digital image)

Scanner (optional)

Printer (optional)

Transfer method (tear-away stabilizer, iron-on transfer paper, or water-soluble pen and light box method suggested; see pattern instructions)

Pencil or pen (optional)

Tracing paper (optional)

Fabric (size according to your image)

Scissors

Embroidery hoop (size according to your image)

Embroidery Thread (DMC thread shown: 3750/blue)

Size 7 embroidery needle

TIME: VARIES WITH LEVEL OF DETAIL AND SCALE OF YOUR IMAGE, BUT APPROXIMATELY 1 TO 4 HOURS FOR A 3- TO 5-IN/7.5- TO 12.5-CM PIECE

1 Choose a picture. This could be as simple as some of your child's handwriting, a drawing, or even a family photograph. Once you find your source material, consider the size of your final piece. Do you want it to be at actual size, smaller, or larger? If you'd like to keep it at its actual size, skip step 2.

2 Scan your image to adjust the size. If you don't have access to a scanner, this can also be done using a copy machine and adjusting the scale. A black-and-white copy is fine; you can reference the original image for color.

3 Transfer the image onto your fabric piece using your desired transfer method (see Transferring & Personalizing Patterns, page 15). An easy, fun option is to use iron-on transfer paper for images that have dense blocks of color and lots of detail. Follow the manufacturer's instructions for printing and transferring the image. The printed transfer

image must be in reverse if there is text, so that it is not backward on the fabric. Embellish the image by outlining the shapes, add small stitches into dense areas of color to create texture, or add new elements.

> TIP: A downside to iron-on transfers is that they create a glossy, almost waxy surface. So cut out the transfer very close to the lines of the image before ironing it onto the fabric. If there are several elements, cut each out separately, and rearrange them on the fabric before ironing. Or fill the hoop with the transfer image, so that the surface is uniform in appearance.

4 Tracing your original image directly onto tear-away stabilizer paper is a great way to make a pattern, too. But don't use a Sharpie, because you may end up with permanent marks on your original material. Use a pencil or light pen marks when tracing over your original material onto the stabilizer. Be sure to move the stabilizer pattern around to combine elements in the original into your pattern. For example, in the sample piece, the funny little dude and signature were not originally together. I added the signature by first tracing the figure, then moving my tear-away stabilizer over the signature, centering it, and tracing.

5 Another transfer method is to use the water-soluble pen method. Using a photocopy or tracing paper template, trace the imagery onto your fabric with the aid of a light box or sunny window (see Transferring & Personalizing Patterns, page 15).

6 Stitch the piece by mimicking the original, or get creative. I tried to follow the original by keeping the lines just as they were, in thickness and density. I used the backstitch and long and short stitches as well as the satin stitch for the hair.

7 Finish your piece by mounting it in an embroidery hoop or frame (see Finishing Techniques, page 132).

LITTLE SILHOUETTES

Silhouettes pull on my heartstrings—they evoke a spirit of nostalgia and Victorian romanticism. Traditional silhouette portraits were made either by tracing a person's shadow or from sight, cutting the shape by hand, which is incredible to imagine. The myth of the Corinthian Maiden portrays the sweet longing that resides in a silhouette. She is attributed with the invention of art by tracing her lover's candlelit silhouette onto a wall to keep him close after he left on a long journey.

This project is inspired by the tradition of papercut portraits and uses your own source materials to make it special. The elongated frame is borrowed from traditional silhouette portraits and allows for lots of flexibility. And remember: you're not limited to a profile image. Think about silhouetting the full length of your child (or anyone, even a family pet!), which would work really well for creating templates from standard-size snapshots. This project looks detailed, but it is actually very easy to make.

Materials

Silhouette Template

Alphabet Template 5

Printed photograph, digital image, or photocopy

Ruler

Tracing paper

Pencil and eraser

Transfer method (transfer paper or water-soluble pen and light box method suggested; see pattern instructions)

7-by-12-in/17.5-by-30.5-cm fabric piece, ironed

Wonder Under

Extra Fine Point Sharpie

Iron

6-by-6-in/15-by-15-cm fabric piece, ironed (for silhouette appliqué)

Scissors

Tweezers

5-by-9-in/12.5-by-23-cm embroidery hoop

9-in/23-cm embroidery hoop (optional)

Pellon Stitch-N-Tear or Sulky Stiffy Stabilizer (optional)

Embroidery Thread (DMC threads shown: 310/black, 3865/white)

Size 5 embroidery needle

Fabric glue

TIME: 2 TO 3 HOURS

1 Dig though your old pictures to find one you'd like to reproduce here, or take a few pictures of your subject in profile. (Have the subject pose against a brightly lit window, so that the profile features are contrasted with the bright background.) Use the Silhouette Template to help compose the size of your image. Enlarge as desired. Print out or photocopy the image.

2 Create your customized text using the Silhouette Template and Alphabet Template 5. Trace the template and gray text guidelines with a ruler onto a sheet of tracing paper. Layer your tracing paper over the alphabet pattern, line up the bottom of your desired letters on the guideline, and trace. This cursive alphabet is really helpful for lining up letters since they will connect to each other, so you don't need to worry about spacing.

3 Transfer your tracing paper pattern onto your fabric using your favorite transfer method (see Transferring & Personalizing Patterns, page 15). Both the transfer paper and water-soluble pen methods would work well here.

4 Trace the silhouette onto the smooth side of the Wonder Under using a fine point Sharpie. Include as many details as you can—like eyelashes, hair, and clothing wrinkles—but for extremely detailed areas it's fine to generalize.

TIP: For creating your silhouette piece with Wonder Under, remember that you need to reverse the image in order for it to be correctly oriented. But this is only important if you want the face to point a certain direction.

5 On a hot, dry setting, iron the rough side of the Wonder Under to the wrong side of the appliqué fabric. Press the Wonder Under for 5 to 8 seconds, then set it aside and let cool. Using a sharp pair of scissors, cut out the silhouette. Peel off the paper backing of the Wonder Under, using tweezers to help separate the paper from the fabric. If you are finding it difficult to remove, press the piece again for a few more seconds and try again. The paper backing should come off cleanly from the fabric, leaving a shiny, smooth surface. Trim any loose, frayed bits of fabric around the edge. You want the silhouette to be sharp and well defined.

6 Place the silhouette onto the background fabric and arrange as you like. Once you have the layout you like best, iron the silhouette appliqué piece to the background fabric. The iron should be on a dry, wool setting and pressed firmly for 10 to 15 seconds or until the two fabrics are fused. Heavier fabrics will require more pressing time. You can also turn your background fabric over and press from the reverse side to ensure fusion.

7 Mount your fabric in an embroidery hoop. I find that oval hoops don't hold fabric as taut as circular hoops do. Using a stabilizer helps. You can also use a 9-in/23-cm embroidery hoop to stitch with, then frame the piece in an oval hoop.

8 Stitch the custom text in a 6-ply backstitch, and stitch the border in a 6-ply coral knot. Easy, easy.

9 Finish your piece either by mounting it in an oval hoop or framing it. To secure the piece in a hoop, cut a ½-in/12-mm fabric allowance from the edges at the back of the hoop and cut away all stabilizer. Glue the fabric allowance to the hoop. (See Finishing Techniques, page 132, for more ideas.) Your piece is ready to hang!

hank

BABY BANNER SAMPLER

Every new baby needs their name embroidered in a banner—they just do. It's like a royal declaration of a new life. This modern take on a birth announcement is a great gift for new parents and nurseries. My mom still keeps the little canvas needlepoint my aunt made for her when I was born. This piece can be a timeless reminder of a little face and a time of great happiness. The banner is left blank for you to fill in a name, a date, or anything you like in your own handwriting to make it that much more personal.

I've worked the piece with printable cotton, a thin sheet of fabric that can be run through your home printer, but feel free to experiment with ink-jet iron-on transfer paper. Just make sure you get one that's appropriate for your dark or light fabric: Some ink-jet iron-on papers are specific to light or dark fabrics.

Materials

Baby Banner Sampler Template

Photograph or digital image

Scanner (optional)

Ink-jet printer

Ink-jet fabric sheets (shown: The Electric Quilt Company)

Iron-on transfer sheets (optional)

Scissors

Tracing paper

Pencil or Extra Fine Point Sharpie

Ruler

Transfer paper

Painter's tape

Dull pencil, pen tip, or tracing stylus

Wonder Under

Iron

Rotary blade (optional)

10-by-10-in/25-by-25-cm (framed in hoop) or 12-by-12-in/30.5-by-30.5-cm (art board/canvas) fabric piece, for background

Tear-away stabilizer (optional)

9-in/23-cm embroidery hoop

Awl or safety pin

Embroidery Thread (DMC threads shown: 822/white, 3773/pink, 501/green, 3740/purple)

Size 7 embroidery needle

8-by-8-in/20-by-20-cm frame or canvas for framing (optional)

TIME: 6 TO 8 HOURS

1 Scan a photograph (at 300 dpi or more) or use a digital image, and size it for the template. The pattern image area is about 5¼ by 5¾ in/13 by 14.5 cm. Feel free to use another image size if you wish. You can easily expand or reduce the size of the pattern to match your image size in a later step by extending or shortening the length of the straight lines at the top and sides of the template.

2 Print the image onto an Ink-jet fabric sheet (or iron-on transfer sheet) following the printable fabric manufacturer's instructions. Let the image dry before handling.

3 Cut out the image leaving a ½-in/12-mm border, and peel off the plastic backing. Set aside.

4 Create your pattern. Trace the pattern template with a pencil or Sharpie onto a sheet of tracing paper. Use a ruler for straight lines. To expand or reduce the size of your image, just adjust the length of the straight lines on the top and sides of the pattern. Start by tracing the corners of the template. Match them up to your image size, and then extend or shorten the length of the border as needed.

5 Prepare the image for the template. Layer the traced pattern over the printed photograph as you like. Then place a sheet of transfer paper between the tracing paper and the photograph. Tape down all layers with painter's tape and transfer the topmost line of the banner where it overlaps the printed photograph (we will cut this away later). Use a dull pencil, pen tip, or tracing stylus.

6 Cut a piece of Wonder Under that extends just beyond the area of the printed image but not to the border of your printable cotton piece (you don't want the Wonder Under to extend beyond the fabric and fuse to your iron). With a hot, dry iron, iron the rough side of the Wonder Under to the wrong side of the printed photograph. Press the Wonder Under for 5 to 8 seconds, then let the piece cool.

7 Cut along the top banner line, creating the negative space of where the banner will be embroidered. Then cut the edges of the printed photograph. You can use scissors, or a rotary blade and ruler for more precise cuts. Make sure your ruler is firmly in place and that the blade is on the side of the ruler opposite of your photograph.

8 Peel the paper backing off the Wonder Under and lay the piece onto your background fabric. Arrange the photograph as desired and iron the photograph appliqué piece to background fabric. The iron should be on a dry, wool setting and pressed firmly for 10 to 15 seconds or until fabrics are fused. You can also turn your background fabric over and press from the reverse side. Let cool.

9 Now transfer the full pattern onto the combined fabrics with the tear-away-stabilizer method or the transfer paper method (see Transferring & Personalizing Patterns, page 15). Water-soluble pen would be difficult to remove on the printed photographic paper. If you use the transfer paper method, just note that you should not transfer the full leaf (if you want to keep the shape closed, feel free to mark the full shape as a guide for stitching) and lazy daisy guides. For the lazy daisy, just mark the bottom and top of each individual petal. For the leaf, mark the top, bottom, and a few guides along the sides of the leaf. You don't want marks visible on the photograph after stitching.

10 Mount your fabric in your hoop and stitch your piece. The tight weave of the printable fabric makes it a little difficult to embroider. I used an awl to prepunch holes, but you can also use a safety pin. Pay extra attention to the corners of the printed photograph, so that you don't pull up the image by tugging too hard on your embroidery thread. Here's what I did:

BANNER: 6-ply split stitch.

NAME: 4-ply split stitch.

BORDERS: 2- and 4-ply backstitch.

FLOWERS: 6-ply lazy daisy stitch.

LEAVES: 4-ply open fishbone stitch.

FLOWER CENTERS: 6-ply French knots in a cluster.

11 Finish your piece by mounting it in a hoop or framing it (see Finishing Techniques, page 132). Your piece is ready to hang!

HOLIDAYS, BIRTHDAYS & SPECIAL

OCCASIONS

PERENNIAL MONOGRAM

There's a lot of love stitched into this little "C" made for my mom, Cecilia. The perennial flowers that wreath the monogram in this piece are a symbol of constant love and affection. If you're looking for a birthday or anytime gift this decorative floral monogram may be just perfect. I had so much fun stitching this pattern, because there are so many different stitches. The pattern is the jumping-off point and the stitch guide is just a suggestion: I encourage you to experiment. Try varying the size of the lazy daisy stitches, adding French knot embellishments around the wreath, or just changing the colors and stitches.

Materials

Perennial Monogram Template

Alphabet Template 6

Transfer method (water-soluble pen and light box method suggested; see pattern instructions)

Water-soluble pen

Painter's tape

7-by-7-in/17.5-by-17.5-cm fabric

5-in/12.5-cm embroidery hoop

Sulky Stiffy stabilizer (optional)

Scissors

Embroidery Thread (DMC threads shown: 832/yellow; 3012/green; 924, 3768/blues; 154/purple; 3834, 316, 223, 3041, 3726, 3740/ purples and pinks)

Size 5 embroidery needle

TIME: 6 TO 8 HOURS

1 Choose your transfer method (see Transferring & Personalizing Patterns, page 15). It's particularly easy to use the water-soluble pen transfer method for transferring this pattern. If you don't have a light box, a sunny window will work just as well. Attach the pattern template to the light box (or window) with painter's tape. Center your piece of fabric over the pattern, and tape down all four sides. Trace the pattern onto the fabric with a water-soluble pen. When the wreath is transferred, tape the script template to the light box and center the letter of your choice within the wreath, tape the fabric and template in place, and trace the letter onto the fabric.

2 Mount the fabric in an embroidery hoop. If you'd like a sturdier stitch surface, use a stabilizer behind your fabric, like I did. Both the fabric and stabilizer should be pulled smooth and taut. It's time to stitch! Here's what I did:

LARGER FLOWERS: 6-ply satin stitch. Feel free to work with 4- or even 2-ply for smooth delicate stitches but that means a lot of stitches, and 6-ply thread helps to fill in the flowers faster. You can also skip the satin stitch and simply outline the flower shape in a backstitch, split stitch, or chain stitch.

> **TIP:** Don't tie knots at the ends of thread lengths while working this dense satin stitch. Knots make it difficult to stitch through. Instead, leave a thread length of about 3 in/7.5 cm as you begin to stitch. Hold this to the side as you stitch so it doesn't tangle into your stitches. After you've made a bunch of satin stitches, you can rethread this thread length onto your needle and tuck it under and around previous stitches. You can also stitch over this thread length as you make your satin stitches to hold it in place. Snip off the remaining length of thread.

For each flower in the wreath, there are three rings. Satin stitch the two outer rings in different colors. Start with the largest, outermost ring. Bring your needle up through the fabric at the outer edge of the flower and drop it down at the inner edge of the ring.

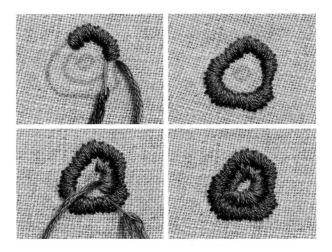

Follow this pattern to create a smooth ring of satin stitches. Feel free to let the shapes be organic—your stitches can extend beyond the flower rings.

> **TIP:** Working in a circle on the flower rings, you may find that the stitches bunch up and don't evenly cover the space. You can fan out the stitches at the outer edge, letting some of the fabric show through. Or every few stitches, you can go back into your previous entry point at the inner edge of the ring, or the previous stitch, and sew another stitch. I doubled and even tripled up on stitches so that the ring filled up evenly.

VINE: 6-ply split stitch.

LEAVES: 6-ply open fishbone stitch.

> **TIP**: To create the curvy leaves in the open fish-bone stitch, it's helpful to create a "bent" stitched guideline down the center of the leaf shape.

SMALL FLOWERS: 6-ply lazy daisy stitch. Note that the template drawing is just a guide for where the flowers might go, but the length, exact placement, and loopiness of the petals is up to you. I cut about 24 in/ 61 cm of thread per two flowers. I suggest not stitching more than two flowers per thread length, because the threads fray quickly with this stitch.

LARGE FLOWERS, CENTERS: 6-ply French knots. I bunched up two to three knots per flower and jumped from flower to flower (behind the fabric) with my working thread. If you are making a piece that is not mounted or doesn't have a backing, like a tea towel, for example, then you'd want to tie a knot and start a new thread length for each flower.

CENTRAL MONOGRAM: 6-ply chunky chain stitch, doubled up at the widest portions of the monogram to create an elegant, curvy letter. Start at the bottom and work up in a single line of chain stitches. Follow the guide marks just inside the guideline. At the two ends of the letter, pull your stitches a bit tighter, to taper the stitches at the ends. Start the second row of chain stitches where the letter begins to widen. Place the stitches close to the first line of chain stitches and then move them farther out as the letter widens, making sure the two lines still touch. Once all the lines are complete, you can blend the two lines together by adding some straight stitches from the outer line into the inner line.

3 Remove any visible water-soluble pen marks by lightly spraying with water or gently rub with a damp cloth.

4 Finish your piece either by mounting it in an embroidery hoop or framing it (see Finishing Techniques, page 132). The piece is ready to hang!

STITCHED CARDS

I can't remember every gift I've received, but I always keep the cards. I love to sift through my shoebox of cards when I need a little pick-me-up and reminisce on those celebrations. Sometimes that's all I want—a thoughtful, handwritten card. And handmade? All the better! These card templates go far beyond the ordinary store-bought cards and can be used for all sorts of occasions: birthdays, Mother's and Father's Day, graduations, holidays, little and big milestones, and just because. Try changing the colors for specific occasions, and adding your own embellishments, like stitching the age of the birthday gal or guy on the card with the stitched award ribbon.

You can make you own cards out of card stock or purchase premade blank cards at any stationery or craft store.

Materials

Embroidered Cards Template

Scissors

Paper clips

4½-by-6¼-in/11-by-15.5-cm standard A6 folded card

Three 5-by-7-in/12.5-by-17.5-cm cardboard sheets

Awl or safety pin

Embroidery thread (see instructions)

Size 5 embroidery needle

4½-by-6¼-in/11-by-15.5-cm paper (optional, to cover the working stitches inside the card)

Glue stick (optional, to glue paper over the stitches inside the card)

Thread conditioner (optional, but recommended)

TIME: 30 TO 45 MINUTES FOR EACH CARD

TIP: Try using a thread conditioner, like Thread Heaven or beeswax to smooth threads as they loosen and lose their shine going through the rough paper multiple times.

1 Cut out your template, or make a photocopy and then cut it out. You can use the template over and over again, even after you punch holes in it. Use paper clips to attach the template to the face-up card. Then place the card on several thicknesses of cardboard.

2 Punch a hole in each black dot on the template using an awl, or in a pinch, a safety pin. Keep the holes small: don't punch your awl all the way through the paper. Remember, when you are punching the holes, the card should be face up and not folded. When you punch the holes, it creates a burr, so it's better to have this on the inside of the card.

3 Make sure you punched all the holes before removing the template. It can be easy to miss a few. To be sure, hold the template and card together and lift them to a light source. Check to see that light passes through each black dot of the template.

4 Stitch your card. Once you've stitched your card, you can paste in a paper backing to cover your stitches, or let all your hard work show—it's kind of pretty and impressive to see all those stitches.

Now, let's make your cards!

AWARD RIBBON CARD (DMC thread colors shown: 725/yellow, 3847/teal)

1 Start with the circle, using a 6-ply backstitch. Tie a knot at the end of an 18-in/46-cm length of thread in your desired color. To start, come up from below, or from the back side (inside) of the card, at any point along the circle, and use the backstitch to complete the circle.

2 To end a thread length, on the back side tuck the working thread under a few stitches, then tie a knot and snip off the ends.

3 For the ribbons, use a 6-ply backstitch. You'll need two 18-in/46-cm lengths of thread. It's best to use two lengths of thread rather than one very long thread, because the paper will strip the thread of its sheen and will unravel it. Begin at the top left point where the ribbon meets the pinwheel shape.

4 For the pinwheel ribbon, use a 6-ply backstitch. Use two 28-in/71-cm lengths of thread. Begin at point A and follow this diagram using a backstitch.

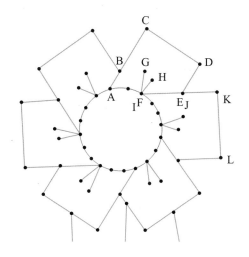

HAPPY BIRTHDAY CARD (DMC thread colors shown: 413/gray, 937/green, 3685/mauve)

To complete this card, you only need to use the backstitch. So easy! You can use different thread colors for each letter or keep it simple and use one or two different thread colors for each word.

1 Tie a knot at the end of a length of thread in the desired color. The thread length will depend on the number of letters you plan to stitch: 6 to 18 in/15 to 46 cm. Start by coming up from the back side, or inside, of the card, and work the stitches from left to right.

2 To end a thread length, on the back side of the card tuck the working thread under a few stitches, tie, and cut.

GET WELL CARD (DMC thread color shown: 321/red)

Just like the Happy Birthday card, you only need the backstitch for this card. Super easy!

1 For each line, I used a different length of thread, 12 to 16 in/30.5 to 40.5 cm long. Tie a knot at the end of a length of thread in the desired color. Start by coming up from the back side, or inside, of the card, and work stitches from left to right.

2 To end a thread length, on the back side of the card tuck the working thread under a few stitches, tie, and cut.

LAUREL WREATH CARD (DMC thread colors shown: 937/green, 938/brown)

1 First embroider the oval shape, then the leaves. You'll need two lengths of 6-ply thread: one for the oval and one for the leaves. Tie a knot at the end of a length of 18-in/46-cm thread in the desired color. Start by coming up from the back side, or inside, of the card, and work the stitches from left to right.

2 To end a thread length, on the back side of the card, tuck the working thread under a few stitches, tie, and cut.

LAZY DAISY FLOWERS CARD (DMC thread colors shown: 597/blue, 733/olive green, 758/peach, 3820/yellow)

This card is tricky but fun. The lazy daisy stitch is easy to do on fabric, but a bit pesky on paper, and there are many more holes to this pattern. To begin, punch the holes with the awl, but enlarge the center points of the flower to about ¼ in/6 mm by rolling the awl in a circular motion. After you remove the template from the card, keep it close by, so that you can follow the pattern.

1 Start with the flowers. Tie a knot at the end of a 14-in/35.5-cm length of thread. From the center point of a flower, come up from the back side, or inside, of the card and down again in the center creating a loop. Hold the knotted end length in place on the back side as you make your first stitch, because the center hole is large enough that you could easily pull the knot through. Holding the loop in place, come up from an outer petal point and lace your needle through the loop. Now anchor the loop in place by coming back down into that same outer petal point. You've made one flower petal. Repeat this process to complete each petal. Once the flower is complete, tie the working thread to the beginning knotted length of thread to secure the threads in place. But don't tug too hard.

2 If the embroidery thread becomes loose as you stitch, just keep going. When you're done, you can use your needle to push loose threads toward the center point of the flower and down.

3 Once the flowers are complete, stitch the leaves, using the same loop and anchor method.

4 To end a thread length, on the back side of the card, tuck the working thread under a few stitches, tie, and cut.

STITCHED GIFT TAGS

If wrapping packages is your forte, then these embroidered gift tags are for you! It's all about the presentation, so just imagine your duly impressed recipient as they see your sweet package with a handmade tag. The tags range from super simple to wow-I-just-made-that! And most require little more than the backstitch to complete. I hand-cut the tags out of colored card stock (you can make several tags from a single sheet of card stock), but you can also use the embroidery patterns on store-bought shipping tags, for a truly fast and fun DIY project.

Materials

Gift Tag Template(s)

Paper clips

Card stock or premade shipping tags

Ruler

X-ACTO knife

Mat board

Scissors

Bone folder

Hole punch

Three 5-by-7-in/12.5-by-17.5-cm pieces of cardboard

Awl or safety pin

Embroidery Thread (DMC threads shown: Hello: 351/coral, 352/light coral, 746/light yellow, 972/yellow; Open Me: 598/light blue, white; Oval with rays: 3820/yellow; To-From: (large, red) 307/yellow, 993/aquamarine; Candy Cane: 890/green, 3865/off white; Yellow Tags: 304/red, 311/navy; To-From: (small, kraft) 3820/yellow, 3847/teal; Anchor: 3865/cream; Heart and Arrow: (large, light blue) 321/red, 3865/off white; Stars: 972/yellow; Heart and Arrow: (small, purple) 304/red, 729/yellow; Large Kraft Tag: 349/red, 3820/yellow)

Size 5 embroidery needle

Thread conditioner (optional)

Thread or ribbon for tag loops

TIME: 15 TO 30 MINUTES PER TAG, IF YOU'RE MAKING THE TAGS FROM SCRATCH

1 Cut out your individual tag template(s). You can also make a photocopy of the template to save the original template or to increase the scale. You can use this template over and over again, even after you punch holes in it.

2 Using paper clips, attach the template to the card stock or premade tag. Use the ruler and the X-ACTO knife to cut out the tag shape on mat board, or you can cut out the tag shape with scissors. Remember to double the size of the tag so you have a front and back. Then, mark the tag along the centerline using the template. Remove the template and score this line with a ruler and a bone folder, and fold the tag. The folded tag covers the back of the tag and gives you more room to write. Using the template as a guide, make a hole with the hole punch through both sides of the tag near the top.

3 Line up and paper clip the template with the open, face-up tag and place on a stack of cardboard. Hold the tag in place as you punch holes with the awl. Remove the paper clip.

4 Stitch the tag using the backstitch. Start each thread length with a knot. To end a thread length, tuck the working thread under a few stitches on the back side of the tag, tie a knot, and cut.

TIP: Use French knots for the exclamation point and the colons. You can come up and go down through the same hole. Since the card stock is thick, the knot won't come through if you don't pull too hard.

TIP: Use contrasting thread colors for the whipped stitch to create the candy cane stripes.

5 Finish off the tag by folding it and lacing an 8-in/20-cm thread or ribbon through the punched hole, and tie it into a loop.

SNOWFLAKE ORNAMENT

A winter snowfall is something I never thought I'd look forward to. Growing up in perpetually sunny Southern California, I hardly experienced the seasons. I thought winter ended in December when all the TV programs stopped airing their holiday shows. When I moved to upstate New York, I learned that this is not at all the case. While I may never fully acclimate to blustery winters, I do love the snow. Nothing is more seasonal for me than white, blanketed streets and snowy days. Celebrate the season with this little snowflake ornament, and if you're on the sunnier side of things, these will help you create your own little bit of winter.

Materials

Ornament Template

Tracing paper

Pencil and eraser

Extra Fine Point Sharpie

Ruler

Transfer method (transfer paper or tear-away stabilizer suggested; see pattern instructions)

Water-soluble pen or hot iron transfer pen (optional)

3-in/7.5-cm embroidery hoop

5-by-5-inch/12.5-by-12.5-cm square of fabric, ironed

4-by-4-in/10-by-10-cm piece of Sulky Stiffy or Pellon Stitch-N-Tear stabilizer (optional)

Sewing pins

Embroidery Thread (DMC threads shown: 3865/off white)

Size 5 embroidery needle

Fabric glue

TIME: 2 HOURS

1 First, do you want to create a custom date? If yes, use the template to create the date on a piece of tracing paper. Trace the snowflake and the dashed lines under where your numbers will be to help with spacing. To add numbers for your custom date, line up the straight dashed lines with the bottom of the desired number and trace. You can use a pencil to make the initial marks, and then trace over with an Extra Fine Point Sharpie.

2 Choose your transfer method. If you are going to stitch onto a dark fabric, use the transfer paper method or tear-away stabilizer method (see Transferring & Personalizing Patterns, page 15). For the tear-away method, trace the template with an Extra Fine Point Sharpie onto a piece of Sulky Tear-Away Stabilizer. If you made a custom date, trace that too. Set aside.

For lighter fabrics, any transfer method will work well (water-soluble pen, transfer paper, or iron-on transfer pen or pencil). Transfer the pattern in the medium that is best for you.

3 Mount the fabric in the embroidery hoop. If you'd like a sturdier stitch surface, use a backing stabilizer (Sulky Stiffy/Pellon Stitch-N-Tear) behind your fabric. Both the fabric and stabilizer should be pulled smooth and taut in the embroidery hoop. If you are using the tear-away method, pin your pattern to the mounted fabric with sewing pins, which is how I transferred this pattern.

4 Now let's get to the stitching. Here's what I did:

SNOWFLAKE: 4-ply backstitch. Start from the outermost point of one of the snowflake's arms. Because this shape is not a continuous line, it's okay to jump around a bit. Plus, if you're going to mount it in the hoop, who is going to see?

DATE: 4-ply backstitch.

SMALL STARS: 2-ply cross-stitch and star stitch. Create dimension by varying the length of the star arms and the thread count for a few stars. Do some 4-ply, some 3-, some 2-, and so on. Try different colors, too.

5 A 3-in/7.5-cm embroidery hoop makes the perfect frame for this piece and is easy to hang as an ornament from the hoop's hardware. To secure the fabric to the hoop, cut a ½-in/12-mm fabric allowance from the back of the hoop and cut away all stabilizer. Glue the fabric to hoop (see Finishing Techniques, page 132).

CUSTOM ZODIAC

I wonder what it must have been like to star gaze before big cities burnt out the night sky with their own great lights. How did the ancients see the stars? Clearly enough to imagine that they saw great beasts, sea goats, centaurs, and winged ladies. Inspired by these zodiac myths, I've made this project to look like the star maps of old. Each zodiac constellation is represented in its mythological shape and with the constellation's stars in place. Stitch this up for a perfect birthday gift!

The pattern is drawn in a continuous line, but using a simple running stitch creates the dashed lines iconic to old star maps. This is the only project in the book where I used a thread other than DMC thread. I used Sajou, a fancy, fine, 4-ply cotton embroidery thread made in Paris. The light yellow (Sajou 2042) color was too perfect to pass up (see Resources, page 134).

Materials

Zodiac Template

Transfer paper (optional)

Tear-away stabilizer (recommended for dark fabrics)

Pencil and eraser (optional)

Extra Fine Point Sharpie (optional)

Sewing pins (optional)

6-by-6-in/15-by-15-cm fabric piece, ironed

4-in/10-cm embroidery hoop

Embroidery thread (thread shown: Sajou 2042)

Size 5 embroidery needle

Scissors

Tweezers

TIME: 2 TO 4 HOURS

1 Choose which zodiac sign you'd like to embroider. Photocopy according to the enlargement instructions and transfer the pattern (see Transferring & Personalizing Patterns, page 15). For dark fabrics, use the transfer paper or tear-away stabilizer method. You can trace the template onto your tear-away stabilizer directly from the printed template; just note that a Sharpie might bleed through the stabilizer, marking your printed template, so you might want to use a pencil to trace the pattern instead. For lighter fabrics, feel free to use any transfer method.

2 Mount the fabric in the hoop. If you are using tear-away stabilizer, pin the pattern to the stretched fabric.

3 Stitch! Here's what I did, in sequence:

ZODIAC STARS: 2-ply star stitches in various sizes. Vary the length of the star arms to create sparkle and dimension.

ZODIAC SILHOUETTE: 2-ply running stitch. Keep the lengths as even as possible, with tiny spaces between each stitch.

4 Once you've finished embroidering the pattern, it's time to remove the tear-away stabilizer, which can be a bit tricky. Removing the stabilizer can pull up your stitches if pulled too quickly, so carefully remove it with the help of tweezers, small sharp scissors, and by gently tearing and pulling the edges with your fingers. It helps to start by trimming off the excess with scissors and then move inward by gently tearing close to the stitches, holding the stitches down, and removing any excess tiny bits with tweezers.

5 After you've removed the stabilizer, consider filling in the background with random cross-stitches and star stitches. Vary the thread plies and the size of the stars to create a dimensional, star-filled night sky.

6 Frame your piece in the working embroidery hoop, or use another finishing method (see Finishing Techniques, page 132).

KEEPSAKES & FORGET-ME-NOTS

FAMILY TREE

Making your own embroidered family tree is truly a labor of love. Each life is represented by a unique leaf that can extend beyond the frame of the piece. I'm hoping that eventually I can add some new leaves to my piece, and you will be able to too. Imagine your tree bustling with leaves!

This pattern can be adapted to fit your family by extending the boughs or adding additional branches to the tree. And while it's a lot of fun to make the leaves three-dimensional and bendable, you can simplify the pattern and cut out much of the making time by stitching the leaves and names right onto the background fabric.

Materials

Family Tree Template

Alphabet Template 2

Ruler

Pen

Extra Fine Point Sharpie

Tracing paper

Transfer method (transfer paper or water-soluble pen and light box method suggested; see pattern instructions)

Fabric for leaves, size dependent on number and size of leaves (two different cotton fabrics shown)

Backing fabric, for added strength (optional)

6-in and 8-in/15-cm and 20-cm embroidery hoops

Embroidery Thread (DMC threads shown: 581, 937/moss greens, 890/dark green, 3865/off white, 300/red brown)

Size 7 embroidery needle

22-gauge craft wire

Wire cutter (I used a Kobalt cutter)

Round-nose pliers (optional)

Thread conditioner (optional)

Scissors

Fray Check

10-by-10-in/25-by-25-cm piece of fabric (for the background)

Sewing pins

TIME: VARIES DEPENDING ON THE NUMBER OF TREE BRANCHES AND LEAVES. EACH LEAF TAKES 1½ TO 2 HOURS AND THE STANDARD TEMPLATE TAKES 2 TO 4 HOURS.

1 First let's trace the leaves. Using a ruler and a pen or Sharpie, draw a straight line across the tracing paper. Place the tracing paper over the alphabet template. Line up the bottom of the alphabet letters with the straight line you drew. Trace the letters of your choice. Space the letters evenly apart.

2 Layer your tracing paper over the leaf pattern shapes. Choose an appropriate-sized leaf for each name. Trace the leaf shape around the name with a Sharpie.

3 Transfer the leaf shapes and the names onto the leaf using your favorite transfer method. The transfer paper and water-soluble pen methods work well here (see Transferring & Personalizing Patterns, page 15).

4 Stitch your leaf names. Mount your fabric in the smaller embroidery hoop. I used a backing fabric for added strength, but this is optional. Increasing the layers adds resistance when you stitch, which can make embroidering more difficult. Stitch the names in a 6-ply backstitch. Stitch all the names, starting a new length of thread for each name.

5 Using wire cutters, cut a 6-in/15-cm length of craft wire for each leaf.

6 Use the craft wire to make the leaf shapes one at a time. Form a length of wire with your fingers or round-nose pliers to match the shape of the leaf. It doesn't have to be exact. Attach the wire to the fabric by making single straight stitches from the back of the fabric, around the wire, and back into the same hole or close to it. Do this along the leaf outline about every centimeter, following the leaf's outline. Make any adjustments to the wire with your fingers. As you stitch, the wire will be pulled into the correct shape. Cut off any excess wire with wire cutters. Continue this process until each leaf is outlined in wire (see images, facing page).

7 Satin stitch a border around the leaf shape to cover and lock the wire into place. Keep the satin stitches about 1/4 in/6 mm long, close together, smooth, and with a uniform edge. You may need to sew a few extra stitches to cover up where the two wire ends meet. Thread conditioner will help if you find your thread is being less than cooperative in this tight satin stitch.

8 Cut each leaf shape out with small, sharp fabric scissors. Cut close to the edge without snipping the stitched threads. Remove any water-soluble pen marks with water. Seal the edges of the leaf with Fray Check, which will also help if you accidentally cut (like I did—oops!) any of the satin stitches.

9 Using the Family Tree pattern and the alphabet template, create your family tree, customized with your family name. Use the guidelines and alphabet as described in step 1.

10 Transfer the tree pattern to the fabric using your favorite transfer technique.

11 Mount your fabric in the 8-in/20-cm embroidery hoop and get stitchin'. Here's what I did:

TREE: 6-ply split stitch. Keep the stitches somewhat jagged for an organic feeling.

FAMILY NAME: 6-ply backstitch.

Hold off on stitching the small leaves along the boughs until after you've attached the leaves with the names.

12 Lay the leaves on your background fabric and arrange them into a composition you like. Pin the leaves to the fabric. Stitch only one corner of the leaf to the background fabric with 3-ply satin stitches in the same embroidery thread used for the border of the leaf. Come up from the back of the fabric with your needle, piercing the back of the leaf along the satin stitches, and from there loop around the leaf and drop the needle straight down into the fabric. Make 5 to 10 of these stitches to lock the leaf in place at the stem end. Repeat this process until all the leaves have been stitched into place.

13 The final touch is the tiny leaves along the tree boughs. A variety of 2- and 3-ply straight and detached chain stitches in alternating colors give a touch of texture, color, and life to any leafless tree limbs.

14 Good job on your finished piece! But remember this is a work in progress. I hope that your tree grows with your family, as you add new leaves and names

to it. Finish your piece by mounting the embroidery in your working hoop or in a frame (see Finishing Techniques, page 132). Your family tree is ready to display!

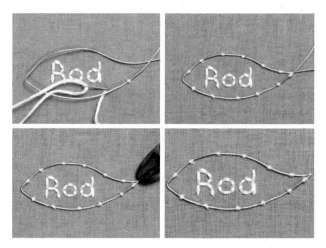

7

The Best Things Come
in Small Packages

PAPER & TYPE

This project combines some of my favorite old-timey materials: vintage book paper and typewritten text. I love the aged patina of old book paper, the serendipitous words scattered on a single loose page, and the rough edges of typewriter text. Choose supple paper for this project. Paper that is brittle will be too difficult to work with.

You can use this method to stitch on all types of papers—maps, illustrations, photographs. Plot the course of a trip on a map, embellish a beloved old book page, or just frame decorative papers in embroidery hoops. A plastic hoop works best to begin with when you mount and stitch, and then you can frame the finished piece in a wooden hoop.

Materials

Alphabet Template 7

Paper (for embroidering)

5-by-7-in/12-by-17.5-cm piece of tight-weave, neutral-colored fabric (cotton suggested)

Iron

4¾-by-6¾-in/12.5-by-17-cm sheet of Wonder Under

Scissors

Tweezers (optional)

Foam brush

Matte Mod Podge

Extra Fine Point Sharpie

Tracing paper

Pencil and eraser

Painter's tape

Bone folder (optional)

Two 3-in/7.5-cm embroidery hoops, plastic and wooden

Embroidery Thread (DMC threads shown: 310/black, 3777/red)

Size 7 embroidery needle

Fabric glue or glue gun (optional)

TIME: 1 TO 2 HOURS

1 Prepare your paper for embroidering. Choose a tight-weaved, smooth, neutral piece of fabric to back your paper. A light-colored cotton would be best; it will add strength once fused to the paper, and it won't show through. Iron the rough side of the sheet of Wonder Under to the fabric with a hot, dry iron. The Wonder Under piece should be a bit smaller than your fabric piece. Press the Wonder Under for 5 to 8 seconds, and set aside to cool.

2 Peel the paper backing from the Wonder Under. Tweezers are helpful if the backing proves tricky to remove. Try bending the corner of the fabric. Now, iron the fabric with the fused Wonder Under backing to the wrong side of your paper. Make sure the Wonder Under does not extend beyond the paper edges, or you could accidentally fuse the paper to your iron or ironing board. Press with a hot, dry iron for about 10 to 15 seconds. Let cool.

3 Using a foam brush, apply a smooth, even coating of Mod Podge over the front of the paper item. A generous coating will add strength and flexibility to the paper. Brush strokes may be visible once the surface is dry, so make sure your strokes are even to minimize their appearance. Set aside to dry.

4 Create your custom pattern. Trace the letter of your choice with a Sharpie onto tracing paper.

NOTE: This project is for one letter in a 3-in/7.5-cm embroidery hoop, but you can also stitch a full word by using a larger piece of paper and hoop.

5 Flip the tracing paper over, so that your letter is now in reverse, and retrace the letter with a soft pencil. We're going to use the pencil marks to rub onto the dry Mod Podge paper, so feel free to color in the letter with pencil to help guide your stitching.

6 Transfer the letter. Tape the pencil tracing face down over the dry Mod Podge paper. Rub over the letter shape with a bone folder, fingernail, or a hard blunt surface to transfer the graphite letter. Lift the tracing paper at the edge to see if the lines are being transferred, and keep rubbing until the letter is fully transferred.

7 Now we're ready to hoop the paper, which can be a bit tricky since the paper is stiff. A plastic hoop works best to begin with. First, center the letter over the inner frame of the hoop. Start smoothing the paper around the hoop shape with your hands. Once the paper has an impression of the bottom hoop, place the outer hoop over it and lightly push down. Don't force the hoop down or you may rip the paper. Remove the outer hoop, tighten the hardware a bit, and place the hoop over the paper again, pushing down slowly and smoothing out the paper. Do this a few times, making an impression on the paper until you are able to push

the hoop down all the way. Your working surface should be smooth and taut.

8 Stitch your letter in a 4-ply satin stitch. Start and end the stitch lengths as if stitching normally on fabric. Stitching on paper is less forgiving than fabric—anywhere you enter the paper, or pierce the paper with your needle, will be visible. Make your entry points into the paper as precise as possible. When coming up from the back of the piece and searching for where to enter the paper, have your needle pierce inside of the pencil guidelines, and move your needle out if needed.

NOTE: Entering the paper from the back pushes the paper up, causing a bump, whereas going down into the paper from the front makes a smoother edge. To minimize this effect, work your satin stitches at a 45-degree angle, wrapping around the pencil guidelines. For a smooth look, try to have the smooth edge on the outside of your letter. You can push any bumpy edges down with a bone folder or your fingernail.

9 Since the paper will now be molded to the shape of your hoop, the best finishing option is to mount it into an embroidery hoop of the same size (or frame within a mat smaller than the hoop size). If you were working with a plastic hoop, feel free to switch to a wooden hoop for framing, which aesthetically goes well with this project. Cut off the paper edges, leaving a ½-in/12-mm allowance at the outer edge of the hoop. Snip into 1-in/2.5-cm-long sections and attach to the inner hoop with fabric glue or a glue gun. You can also just cut the paper fabric close to the edge of the hoop and seal that edge with glue. Your embroidery is ready to hang!

LOVED ONE'S SIGNATURE

My namesake is my paternal grandpa, Jesse. I never got to meet him, but I'm lucky enough to have a bunch of letters that he wrote to my grandmother. For this project, I used the handwritten closing from one of his letters as an embroidery pattern. I followed his pencil lines as best I could, tracing with needle and thread the marks he had made almost seventy years ago. It feels powerful to weave the past into the present, and this piece will be a cherished memorial for my family.

Your own embroidery piece will vary depending on your chosen source material and scale—just think of all the possibilities. Pull out that old box of letters, cards, photographs, and documents. Maybe there's a scratchy description or date on the back of a photo, a casually penned name on an envelope, your child's earnest signature on a drawing, or just a great line in a letter you'd love to see every day or share with someone special. Any of these, and lots more, would make wonderful material for this project.

Materials

Personal source material

Scanner (optional)

Printer (optional)

Tracing paper

Extra Fine Point Sharpie

Pencil and eraser

Sulky Tear-Away Stabilizer

Water-soluble pen (optional)

Sewing pins

Fabric, size varies (add 2-in/5-cm to hoop size, before mounting to the hoop; my fabric piece was 7-in/17.5-cm square)

Embroidery hoop, size varies (5-in/12.5-cm shown)

Embroidery Thread (DMC thread shown: 844/dark gray)

Size 7 embroidery needle

Tweezers

Scissors

Fabric glue

Staple gun (optional)

TIME: 1 TO 4 HOURS FOR A 3- TO 5-IN/7.5- TO 12.5-CM PIECE, DEPENDING ON THE LENGTH OF YOUR TEXT AND THE SCALE OF THE PIECE

1 After selecting your source material, think about the scale you'd like for it. I enlarged the text to fit within a 5-in/12-cm hoop by scanning the original text and enlarging the words to the desired size. Increasing the scale helps to give definition to the shape of the letters, but it is not necessary. You can also use a copier to enlarge your source material.

2 If you choose to scan your original, scan at a minimum of 300 dpi at 100 percent. If you are going to enlarge your image, scan at a higher resolution (600 dpi), if possible. It also helps to increase the contrast, which may be done in your scanning software or other imaging software, like Photoshop. You can do this with either the Contrast tool or the Levels tool. This step is not necessary as long as the lines of the text are distinct. Size the image according to the hoop size or frame you'd like to finish your piece in.

REMEMBER: A general rule of the thumb for sizing your fabric to embroider on and your pattern: Add 2 in/5cm to the hoop width for fabric size and subtract ¾ in/2 cm from hoop size for final pattern size.

If you choose to use the source material to create a to-scale embroidery, layer a piece of tracing paper over the original and trace the desired lines with an Extra Fine Point Sharpie. Test your tracing paper and Sharpie to make sure that the Sharpie doesn't bleed through and mark your original. If it does, use a pencil first and then retrace the pencil lines with a Sharpie. Once you have the tracing paper copy, use it as your template for transferring your pattern.

3 Whether you enlarge the original or make a tracing paper template, use the tear-away stabilizer transfer method (see Transferring & Personalizing Patterns, page 15), because it allows you to achieve the most accurate details of the original. You can lay the transparent stabilizer material directly over your pattern and trace with a fine point pencil (but beware, pencil can transfer to light-colored threads) or Sharpie to get the details just right. Then, pin the stabilizer onto your stretched fabric in the embroidery hoop. The only trick is removing the stabilizer carefully after you've stitched without disrupting your finished stitches. You can use other transfer methods for this project too.

4 Mount your fabric in the hoop. Stitch with 1- to 3-ply backstitches for even, thin lines. The backstitch is great for text, because it makes smooth, continuous lines. Try to keep your stitches even, a little longer than ¼ in/6 mm, because tiny, short backstitches can look bumpy. To work a curve, shorten your stitches: the tighter the curve, the shorter the stitch.

5 If you used the tear-away transfer method, remove the transfer material now, slowly and carefully. If pulled too quickly, it can also pull up your stitches, so remove carefully by using tweezers, sharp snips, and holding the stitches while gently tearing and

pulling the edges with your fingers. It helps to start by trimming off the excess with scissors and then moving inward, gently tearing close to the stitches and removing any excess tiny bits with tweezers. If you used the water-soluble pen, lightly spray any visible marks with water or rub gently with a damp cloth to remove.

6 Finish your piece either by leaving it in the embroidery hoop and gluing excess fabric to the hoop or stretching over a canvas stretcher and attaching it with a staple gun (see Finishing Techniques, page 132). To secure to hoop, cut a 1/2-in/12-mm fabric allowance from the back of the hoop and cut away all stabilizer. Glue the fabric edges to the back of the hoop. The piece is ready to hang!

NOTE ON FABRIC: To give the aged look of yellowed paper to my natural cotton fabric, I stained the fabric with tea. To do this, in large pot, boil enough water to submerge your fabric. Once the water has boiled, turn off the heat, and add several tea bags of inexpensive black tea. Loosely ball up your fabric and wrap it in rubber bands. Add the fabric ball to the hot tea water and soak for 20 minutes to 1 hour. The longer you leave the fabric in the tea, the darker it will be, and the tighter the ball, the more distinct your crease marks will be, just like in traditional tie-dye.

MESSAGE IN A BOTTLE

"A little magic can take you a long way."
—Roald Dahl, *James and the Giant Peach*

So much wonder and possibility can be contained within a tiny glass bottle. Create a bit of your own magic with this sweet and romantic message in a bottle. The possibilities are pretty much endless: a happy birthday message, a token of love, a bit of a memory scrolled down and bottled up. For this project, I handwrote and stitched some of my favorite romantic quotes onto a scroll of fabric. You can easily make your own text, by writing directly onto your fabric with a water-soluble marker. There are so many different ways to make this project your own. You can also use any of the alphabet fonts in this book.

Materials

Message in a Bottle Template (optional)

Wide-neck bottle with ¾ in/2 cm or wider opening

Cork (to fit the bottle)

4-by-14-in/10-by-35.5-cm fabric strips, prewashed and ironed

Water-soluble pen

Transfer paper (optional)

4-in/10-cm (or larger) embroidery hoop

Embroidery Thread (DMC threads shown: 311/navy, 312/blue)

Size 5 embroidery needle

Scissors

Ruler

Rotary blade

Ribbon

Sewing pins

Sewing machine (optional)

Sewing thread (optional)

Fray Check

TIME: 1 TO 2 HOURS

1 Find a small, wide-neck bottle you'd like to use for this project. Make sure the mouth of the bottle is ¾ in/2 cm or more, so that your fabric scroll can go through it. The longer the scroll, the wider the mouth opening will need to be. Also, base your fabric dimensions on your bottle height.

2 Since these lines of text are long, you'll need the fabric cut into long strips. The narrower you make the fabric strips, the smaller the embroidery hoop will need to be. Leave an extra 2 in/5 cm on the final width of your scroll, so that it will be easy to hoop and embroider. For example, if you'd like your scroll to be 3 by 12 in/7.5 by-30.5 cm, start with a 5-by-12-in/12.5-by-30.5-cm fabric piece. You can also stitch more than one scroll at a time on a larger fabric piece, using a larger hoop.

3 Transfer your desired text directly onto your fabric with a water-soluble pen (see Transferring & Personalizing Patterns, page 15).

4 Mount your fabric in the embroidery hoop, stretching it taut but not so tight that the text is distorted. I don't suggest using a stabilizer for this project since the back will be visible, and it would just add thickness to the scroll. If you really want some added tension to your piece, use a layer of thin cotton fabric behind your embroidery fabric.

5 Stitch! Here's what I did:

TEXT: 3-ply backstitch. Since the back is visible, you'll want to pay more attention than usual to the back of the piece as you stitch. Tie knots to start a length of thread or tuck the beginning length of thread under your stitches (see more on Starting and Ending a Length of Thread, page 20). Don't jump from word to word with your thread. Instead, at the end of a word, tuck the threads under 5 to 6 previous stitches and snip the threads close to the fabric for a clean look. Start each word with a separate length of thread—either use the remaining thread on the needle or start a new length of thread.

6 Once you are done stitching, measure and mark the desired width of your scroll along the length of your fabric with a water-soluble pen and ruler. Use the ruler and rotary blade to cut your scroll length

out. Make sure your rotary blade is on the side of your ruler opposite your embroidery.

7 Add a ribbon to one end of the scroll, which will extend beyond the bottle lip. That way, the scroll can be easily removed from the bottle. Measure the height of your bottle, and add an extra ½ to 1 in/ 12 mm to 2.5 cm length to the piece of ribbon. And if you'd like the ribbon to also wrap around your scroll, add 2 lengths of your scroll width to the final ribbon size.

8 Wrap the ribbon around the scroll edge. Iron and pin place. You can work without a hoop in a simple backstitch to secure the ribbon to one end of the scroll, or you can use a sewing machine like I did. Match your thread color to your ribbon and use a zigzag stitch or a straight stitch to sew along each edge of the ribbon to give it a finished look. Tie off the sewing threads, and then thread them onto a needle and lace the needle under the ribbon edge to hide them under the ribbon.

9 Finish the scroll by sealing the cut, exposed edges of the fabric. Use a bit of Fray Check to seal the fabric edges to keep them from fraying. (Fray Check can possibly change the color of your fabric so test it out first.) Let the fabric dry in the open air, because Fray Check has a strong odor.

10 Roll up your scroll, bottle it up, and give it as a gift or keep it.

PHOTO CORNERS

"And suddenly the memory returns. The taste was that of the little crumb of madeleine."
—Marcel Proust, *Remembrance of Things Past*

It's curious how memory works. For Proust, the taste of a tea-soaked madeleine cookie suddenly, like magic, brings forth childhood memories. Photographs are my madeleines. I love to surround myself with photographs of family and found vintage images too. This project is my new favorite way to display photos. While the project is simple and easy to make, there are endless ways that you can personalize it—the colors you choose for your fabric and photo corners, adding a decorative stitched border (how about the feather stitch and some French knots?), or you can embroider text, like a name, phrase, or date. Handwrite your text directly on the fabric and stitch to make it more special. You can also choose a font from this book.

If you're concerned about working with original images, don't worry. We don't stitch through the images in this project. You may want to consider using a reprint or a photocopy of your image on a thick paper, like card stock, because once the picture is in place, it's tricky to get it out of the photo corners and back in, if you want to ever remove it.

Materials

Photograph or photo reproduction

Fabric, size varies (add 2 in/5 cm to hoop size)

Embroidery hoop, size varies (sizes shown: from 3 in to 5 in/7.5 cm to 12.5 cm)

Pellon Stitch-N-Tear Stabilizer or Sulky Stiffy Stabilizer

Sewing thread

Water-soluble pen

Ruler

Embroidery Thread (DMC thread shown: 3371/dark brown)

Size 5 embroidery needle

Scissors

Q-tip

Fabric glue or glue gun

TIME : 20 TO 30 MINUTES

1 Compose your piece. Arrange your photograph on your fabric and determine which hoop size you will use. Cut a square of fabric and matching square of stabilizer. To determine the size your fabric and

stabilizer should be, add 2 in/5 cm to the hoop size. So, if you have a 3-in/7.5-cm hoop, you'll need a piece of fabric that is 5 in/12.5 cm square.

2 Mount the fabric with stabilizer underneath in the embroidery hoop and create a taut, smooth surface. The stabilizer helps to create a nice, stiff surface that allows you to pull your stitches a bit more than usual, which will help secure your photograph in place while keeping the shape of your photo corners.

3 Temporarily secure the photograph in place with sewing thread. Place the photograph on the fabric where you like it best. With sewing thread, stitch around the center of the photograph, bottom to top, and then, side to side. Sew close to the image edge and secure the thread with a knot. Be careful not to puncture the image or tie the thread too tight, which could pucker or tear the image.

4 Make the photo corner shapes. With a water-soluble pen and ruler, mark small dots on the fabric ½ in/12 mm down the side from each corner of the photograph (2 dots in each of the 4 corners). The dots should be about ⅛ in/3 mm from the edge of the photograph. Then, with ruler and water-soluble pen, make thin, straight lines connecting the 2 dots in each corner to create your 4 photo corner shapes.

5 Stitch the photo corners. I used 6-ply satin stitches. Cut a length of thread 18 in/46 cm long and tie a knot at one end. Be careful not to stitch the actual image

and be sure to keep the ⅛-in/3-mm allowance from the actual edge of the photograph. Work from the widest points, and then follow the water-soluble marks, tapering the satin stitches as you go. Be sure not to stitch too tight or the photograph will pucker. It's best to stitch with the photograph in place. The picture lies flat this way and will be held securely in place.

6 After you stitch the first corner, stitch the opposite, diagonal corner. As you stitch, you may notice that the photograph moves a bit, so working on this diagonal corner will help to keep the photograph in place. Stitch the remaining corners. End each length of thread by tucking it under a few stitches and tying a knot.

7 Remove the temporary sewing thread (not the embroidery thread). Remove water-soluble pen marks with a damp Q-tip if they are still visible.

8 Finish your piece by mounting it in the embroidery hoop (see Finishing Techniques, page 132).

you + me

FINISHING TECHNIQUES

Traditional embroidery is often seen mounted in frames, or sewn on quilts, pillowcases, tea towels, and clothing. The projects in this book take embellishment to another level—home decor with a modern, nostalgic twist—off the tea towel and into the hoop frame. I love framing my stitched pieces in an embroidery hoop. It's not only super convenient, but it looks great, references the creative process, and already has the hardware for hanging built right into it.

EMBROIDERY HOOP

Framing your piece in an embroidery hoop is easy. To start, prep your fabric by removing any water-soluble pen marks or transfer stabilizer. Iron any parts that need to be smoothed out. Try to avoid ironing the actual embroidery. Iron around the stitches or iron the back of the piece.

To create a more finished look, add a backing fabric to cover the back of the embroidery. Cut another piece of fabric similar in size to the original embroidered piece. Center the embroidered image and hoop both fabrics layered together (or you can hoop just the embroidered fabric if you don't mind letting the stitches show on the back side). Smooth out any bumps or puckers on both layers of fabric by pulling gently on the fabric edges. Lay the embroidered piece face down on a clean work surface and cut the fabric around the frame about ½ in/12 mm from the edge (image 1). Cut the fabric edges into small sections, like tabs about 1 in/2.5 cm or so apart (image 2). Secure the tabs to the inner wooden hoop with fabric glue, or for a quick fix, use a glue gun. Paint on the fabric glue

with a small brush and push the tabs of fabric down with your fingers. While fabric glue will dry clear, it can darken the fabric. Make sure to keep your fingers off of the front of the piece and that your work surface is clear of any glue. Fabric glue takes a few hours to dry.

> **TIP:** Stain or paint your wooden hoops to make them look more like frames. Remove the inner embroidery hoop ring and the hardware that tightens the hoop. Set aside. Dip a Q-tip in wood stain and drag it around the hoop and all its edges. Buff the hoop with a rag to remove excess stain and any stain on the metal parts of the hoop. Stained hoops need to dry overnight before you use them. Make sure you are in a well-ventilated area. Delta offers ecofriendly soy-based paint and wood stain options (see Resources, page 134).

FRAME & MAT

To frame your embroidered piece with a mat, iron out any hoop marks on your finished piece. Be careful not to apply too much pressure when ironing, and iron on the back of the piece, or on the edges where there is no embroidery work. If you are framing under glass, make sure that you have a thick enough mat to leave room between the embroidery and the glass, or try a shadow box frame. Cut the embroidered piece about 1 in/2.5 cm smaller than the mat all around. I like to leave room in the fabric if you want to change frames someday. Tape the embroidered piece in place on the back of the mat with linen tape, and place it in the frame. Behind the embroidered piece, layer a thin sheet of batting, foam, or board to help keep the embroidery in place. Then, place the frame's backing on, and hang.

For pieces that need more tension to smooth out hoop marks, stretch the embroidery over a thin sheet of mat board that can fit within your frame. Stretch the embroidery around the mat board and secure in place with linen tape. If there is a window mat in your frame, place it into the frame and then center the stretched embroidery in the windowed mat. Tape in place with linen tape and secure the frame back (images 4 to 7).

CANVAS

You can also display your piece stretched around an artist panel or canvas (either a premade canvas or make your own with stretcher bars). To stretch your piece and smooth out any hoop marks, cut the piece about 2 in/5 cm to 4 in/10 cm (depending on the depth of the artist panel or canvas) larger than the canvas. Lay the piece face down onto a clean work surface. Place the canvas or panel face down, centering the piece. Lift the layers carefully and take a look, to make sure the embroidery is centered, and lay them down again. Use a staple gun to secure one side of the fabric to the back of the frame. Pull evenly (pulling too hard will distort the proportions of the embroidery or make the piece look off-center) and secure the opposite side, making sure that the embroidery is flat and smooth on the front. Fold the corner edges of one side like you are wrapping a present, and secure the corners and length of that side with staples. Finish the remaining corner edges and last side with staples. Then cut any long fabric ends (images 8 and 9).

RESOURCES

I've mentioned specific brands of tools and materials throughout the book, because they work well for these projects. But feel free to substitute other products. Almost all of the tools and materials used in the projects in this book can be found at your local craft, sewing, and hardware stores, and even your local supermarket.

If you live in an area without great craft resources, you may find that it's more convenient to order online for the supplies you need. You can always go in on a large order with friends, and luckily embroidery supplies are relatively inexpensive. But please support your local craft store if you are lucky enough to have one close by.

Stores/Web sites

CREATE FOR LESS
www.createforless.com
This site is basically a craft supply factory at your fingertips. Some items require that you buy in multiples, like embroidery hoops, but the prices are still great. This source is a reliable, go-to for whatever crafty supplies you're seeking. It's especially great for embroidery supplies, Delta Soy Paint and Soy Stain, stabilizer, and general craft supplies.

DICK BLICK
www.dickblick.com
Dick Blick is more oriented to the fine arts, selling paints and brushes, but they also have a lot of craft supplies. It's a great source for glues, transfer paper, brushes, wood artist panels, and stretched canvas.

IKEA
www.IKEA.com
The shadow box frame used in the Key Holder project (page 51) is from IKEA (Ribba, $9.99). They have lots of inexpensive frames that would work well for these projects.

JOANN
www.joann.com
JoAnn is sewing and craft store heaven, and it's been around for ages. I grew up shopping for supplies at JoAnn. As much as I like them, I find that their embroidery supplies can be limited or picked over. Look there for embroidery supplies, fabrics, stabilizer, and general craft supplies.

PURL SOHO
www.purlsoho.com
www.purlbee.com
I feel lucky to live close enough to visit Purl Soho on a regular basis. It's a beautiful store with equally beautiful supplies. Their blog, PurlBee, is also a great resource for inspiration and embroidery how-to. Widely known for their incredible knitting supplies, Purl Soho also stocks fine embroidery threads, embroidery supplies, beautiful fabrics, books, and some general craft supplies.

NEEDLE IN A HAYSTACK
www.needlestack.com/thread/html
To see a huge collection of embroidery threads beyond DMC Embroidery Thread, check out Needle in a Haystack's thread page.

Blogs

SUBLIME STITCHING

www.sublimestitching.com
www.sublimestitching.com/blog

Jenny Hart is the queen bee of embroidery, and her site, Sublime Stitching, offers all sorts of embroidery patterns, embroidery supplies, as well as inspiration and how-tos on her blog.

NEEDLE 'N THREAD

www.needlenthread.com

The Needle 'n Thread blog by Mary Corbet posts embroidery how-tos, tips, and product reviews, as well as current embroidery projects. Her how-to stitch videos and embroidery reference sections are great informative resources.

Books

Barnden, Betty. *The Embroidery Stitch Bible*. Iola, Wisconsin: Krause Publications. 2003.

Bauer, Margie. *The Embroiderer's Handbook*. Newton Abot, England: David & Charles. 2005.

Enthoven, Jacqueline. *The Stitches of Creative Embroidery*. Atglen, Pennsylvania: Schiffer Publishing. 1987.

Gardner, Sue. *A–Z of Embroidery Stitches*. Edwardstown, South Australia: Country Bumpkin Publications. 2002.

Kendrick, Helen Winthorpe. *Stitch-opedia: The Only Embroidery Reference You'll Ever Need*. New York: St. Martin's Griffin, 2010.

Thomas, Mary, and Jan Eaton. *Mary Thomas's Dictionary of Embroidery Stitches*. North Pomfret, Vermont: Trafalgar Square Books. 1998.

INDEX